Going to Pot

Going to Pot

Why the Rush to
Legalize Marijuana
Is Harming America

William J. Bennett
and Robert A. White

CENTER
STREET

New York   Boston

The authors gratefully acknowledge the permission to reprint the chart that appears in the Introduction and the articles that appear in the appendix from:

The New England Journal of Medicine, Nora D. Volkow, Ruben D. Baler, Wilson M. Compton, and Susan R. B. Weiss, "Adverse Health Effects of Marijuana Use," 370, 2219–2227. Copyright © 2014 Massachusetts Medical Society. Reprinted with permission from Massachusetts Medical Society.

The New England Journal of Medicine, "Adverse Health Effects of Marijuana Use," 371, 878–879. Copyright © 2014 Massachusetts Medical Society. Reprinted with permission from Massachusetts Medical Society.

The authors would also like to thank:

Tom Gorman, Director of the Colorado HIDTA (High Intensity Drug Trafficking Area), for his permission to reprint the charts that appear on pages 38, 41, 43, 74, and in the photo insert.

Ben Cort for his permission to reprint the photos that appear on page 51 and in the photo insert.

The chart that appears on page 78 and in the photo insert comes from the National Institute on Drug Abuse (NIDA).

Additional photo permissions:
Bob Berg/Getty Images; Page 46 and photo insert
Seth McConnell/Getty Images; Page 46 and photo insert
Bob Berg/Getty Images; Page 47 and photo insert
Justin Sullivan/Getty Images: Page 52 and photo insert
Bloomberg/Getty Images: Photo insert
Kathryn Scott Osler/Getty Images: Photo insert

Photos on pages 51 (top), 52, 59, photo insert pages 4 (middle and bottom), 7 (bottom), and 8 (top) copyright © 2015 by Hachette Book Group, Inc.

Center Street
Hachette Book Group
1290 Avenue of the Americas
New York, NY 10104

www.CenterStreet.com

Printed in the United States of America

RRD-C

Originally published in hardcover by Hachette Book Group.
First trade edition: February 2016
10 9 8 7 6 5 4 3 2 1

Center Street is a division of Hachette Book Group, Inc.
The Center Street name and logo are trademarks of Hachette Book Group, Inc.

The Hachette Speakers Bureau provides a wide range of authors for speaking events. To find out more, go to www.HachetteSpeakersBureau.com or call (866) 376-6591.

The publisher is not responsible for websites (or their content) that are not owned by the publisher.

Library of Congress data has been applied for.

ISBN 978-1-4555-6073-8 (Hardcover ed.); ISBN 978-1-4789-0373-4 (Audiobook downloadable ed.); ISBN 978-1-4555-6071-4 (Ebook ed.); ISBN 978-1-4555-6070-7 (trade ed.)

We dedicate this book to the men and women who serve on the front lines in the war on drugs at the local, state, and federal level. Their hard work, courage, and sacrifices deserve our gratitude and respect.

Acknowledgments

Together, we would like to thank a talented and devoted group of friends and experts whose thoughts, research, and guidance we could not have done this book without: Dr. Robert DuPont, Dr. Herbert Kleber, Dr. Christian Thurstone, Dr. David Murray, Dr. John Walters, Dr. Casey Wolf, Dr. Bertha Madras, Christopher Beach, Noreen Burns, Alexandra Datig, Ben Cort, Thomas Gorman, Michael Tremoglie, and Steve and Debbie Moak. They all have been at this a long time and, to the degree we can turn around this cultural tide, the nation's thanks will go to all of them.

We would like to express special appreciation to Seth Leibsohn, who has been an integral part of this project from the very beginning.

We also would like to thank Kate Hartson and her team at Hachette Books.

Of course, the love and support of our wives, Elayne and Ginnie, have been invaluable to this project.

Contents

Introduction

We are at a curious, as well as critical, moment in our country. Just when we are spending more than ever on early childhood education (and many are arguing for even more spending), just when we are debating the intellectual and motivational needs of our present and future work force, just as we are concerned about unemployment numbers that are too high (especially in the youth and young adult population), just as we are unveiling a new experiment on universal health care coverage, and just as we are condemning other products deemed unhealthy, like sugars and trans fats, we are—at the same exact time—moving in fact and opinion toward more and more marijuana legalization. We are spending money and political capital on strengthening the health, education, and productivity of our populace, yet society believes it appropriate to push for greater availability of a drug that hinders, and negatively affects (perhaps dramatically), those very efforts.

Over the past several years, as public opinion has moved toward greater acceptance of marijuana, an increasing body of scientific evidence has documented the multiple adverse effects of marijuana use. These serious health issues are detailed in an excellent article produced by the National Institute on Drug Abuse and published in the June 2014 issue of the *New England Journal of Medicine*. We believe this article should be read by everyone, particularly proponents of legalization, and so we have included it in our appendix. The negative consequences of marijuana legalization, particularly those experienced by adolescents, are too crucial to ignore. As you can see from Table 1 of that article, a variety of short- and long-term effects should give pause to anyone who might believe that smoking marijuana is harmless.

Table 1. Adverse Effects of Short-Term Use and Long-Term or Heavy Use of Marijuana

Effects of short-term use

Impaired short-term memory, making it difficult to learn and to retain information

Impaired motor coordination, interfering with driving skills and increasing the risk of injuries

Altered judgment, increasing the risk of sexual behaviors that facilitate the transmission of sexually transmitted diseases

In high doses, paranoia and psychosis

Effects of long-term or heavy use

Addiction (in about 9% of users overall, 17% of those who begin use in adolescence, 25 to 50% of those who are daily users)*

Altered brain development*

Poor educational outcome, with increased likelihood of dropping out of school*

Cognitive impairment, with lower IQ among those who were frequent users during adolescence*

Diminished life satisfaction and achievement (determined on the basis of subjective and objective measures as compared with such ratings in the general population)*

Symptoms of chronic bronchitis

Increased risk of chronic psychosis disorders (including schizophrenia) in persons with predisposition to such disorders

* The effect is strongly associated with initial marijuana use early in adolescence.

Increased Knowledge of the Dangers

On an almost weekly basis, medical researchers, aided by advanced technology not available decades ago, are expanding our knowledge of the negative health consequences of smoking marijuana. As we will discuss in more detail in later chapters, more than smoking tobacco or drinking alcohol, smoking marijuana can damage the heart, lungs, and brain. Moreover, it immediately impairs cognitive abilities and motor coordination, interfering with the smoker's judgment, driving skills, and other basic abilities. Normal development of the adolescent brain is at particularly high risk. Smoking marijuana deposits more tar into the lungs than smoking a cigarette, and there are numerous cancer-causing chemicals in marijuana. There is nearly a fivefold increase in the risk of heart attack in the first hour after smoking marijuana. It is a bitter irony that as our knowledge increases regarding the harm that smoking marijuana does to our health, public perception of those injuries decreases. It is our purpose in this book to inform an uninformed, and sometimes misinformed, public about the true risks of legalization.

Increased Potency

We believe the debate over legalization may, in some places, be the result of two different groups talking past each other. One group, supporting legalization—either tacitly or vociferously—is thinking of the marijuana of low tetrahydrocannabinol (THC) percentiles many people now in their fifties, sixties, and seventies smoked or tried when they were in college, or, for that matter, marijuana they knew from the 1970s and 1980s that was far less potent than today's marijuana (THC being the psychoactive ingredient in marijuana). It may be difficult for people who tried or used a weaker substance to see how legalizing that substance can be so harmful. The problem is that you cannot consider it the same substance when you look at the dramatic increase in potency and the increased negative neurological and other health effects arising from higher THC levels. The point is that there really are two different kinds of marijuana, and thus, perhaps, two different conversations taking place. One is based on a frame of reference of marijuana that was experienced in the past, was weaker, and does not exist today. The other is based on the reality of the marijuana that is grown, processed, and sold today.

Many we have talked to are simply unaware of the potency of today's marijuana. Most who have not smoked or looked at marijuana and its potency in a very long time are surprised to realize that the marijuana they knew in the 1970s or 1980s was *much* less potent than it is now. The levels of THC then were in the low single digits. Today's marijuana THC levels are in the double digits—we've gone from about 3 to 5 percent THC in yesteryear's marijuana to just above 13 percent THC—but common strains are available that go much higher, into the 20 percents and beyond. The difference between 3 to 5 percent THC and 13 to 30 percent THC is very significant. It is like comparing a twelve-ounce glass of beer with a twelve-ounce glass of 80 proof vodka; both contain alcohol, but they have vastly different effects on the body when consumed. Indeed, many argue that because of the difference in potency, it is not even the same drug we once knew. Some have taken to calling today's marijuana "industrial marijuana" or "turbo pot."

For these and many other reasons, it is our view that the effort to legalize marijuana needs to be addressed head on; that if it is not stopped, we will soon look back and ask, "What were we thinking?" We believe marijuana is dangerous and should remain illegal. We also believe most of the arguments in favor of legalization are fallacious. With this book we hope to join a debate over legalization that simply has been too silent, or cowed into silence, on our side. We make no bones about this, as, in short, we think the effort to legalize marijuana is as irrational as any effort to legalize cigarettes would be, were they illegal here.

Engage with us in a hypothetical: assume that cigarettes are not legal and never have been in America, but tens of thousands of packs of cigarettes make it into the United States every year—made in Mexico, Canada, and other countries—and are purchased illegally on the black market. Teenagers and adults smoke them.

Now, imagine there is a bill in Congress to forgo all the enforcement costs of trying to keep cigarettes out of the hands and lungs of Americans by legalizing cigarettes here. Arguments on behalf of cigarette legalization seem to be gaining ground and even make some sense: we would save money on enforcement of the law against selling and smoking cigarettes, we can tax the sales to increase both state and federal revenues, and some doctors even say there can be benefits to smoking (to stave off Alzheimer's disease or decrease stress, for example—which some studies actually support). As some would argue in this scenario, there are no known risks to the brain from nicotine and tobacco inhalation.

Here's the question: with today's understanding of the dangers of cigarette smoking, would you support such hypothetical legislation? Every argument we make was once true of cigarettes; some doctors even recommended smoking and endorsed certain brands of cigarettes. Yes, cigarette sales are taxed at the state and federal levels. And no, we do not see much impairment to the brain from smoking, making it nearly impossible (aside from smell) to discern who, in any given group of people, may have just smoked a cigarette—be that person driving a car, flying an airplane, playing cards, or giving a business presentation.

The Path to Legalization

Of course, given everything we know about the health consequences of smoking tobacco, most people would not vote to legalize cigarettes; now most Americans would oppose such a bill, just as most Americans used to oppose legalization of marijuana. Today that is no longer the case when it comes to marijuana. According to Gallup, nearly 60 percent of Americans favor legalizing marijuana.[1] This is an incredible increase in support for such a proposition, and a first since Gallup began asking such a question. In 1969, a mere 12 percent of Americans thought legalization a good idea. As recently as 2005, still only about one-third of Americans supported legalization. Unfortunately, legalization is no longer a minority position. Such views cross party lines: over 60 percent of Independents and about the same number of Democrats support legalization, while about 35 percent of Republicans do, as well.

The first step on the road to legalization of marijuana started with so-called "medical marijuana." Legalization advocates cleverly and cynically marketed marijuana as a last resort for patients suffering from cancer, HIV, multiple sclerosis, glaucoma, and numerous other maladies. While no scientific studies documented the safety or efficacy of marijuana for these patients, their anecdotal testimony, and its appeal to the public's natural desire to help those in pain, persuaded many that marijuana does have a useful purpose in society. Hence, numerous states, either by legislative action or referendum, created "medical marijuana" legalization programs. Although they were initially designed to provide marijuana to a limited group of patients, in many places this ultimately expanded into actual or de facto recreational use programs with widespread abuse. Some states have more closely regulated structures in place, and the numbers of dispensaries are limited in those locations. However, no doctor in any program actually prescribes marijuana, as is done with every other drug requiring a physician's authorization. Rather, in most states, a doctor gives the patient a note or letter that permits that person to obtain a medical marijuana card. In states such as California and Colorado, well over 90 percent of cardholders simply list "severe pain" as the ailment for which they need the marijuana. The overwhelming majority of these cardholders are males under the age of thirty-five. Much of the purchased "medical marijuana" finds its way into the hands of children and adolescents. Unlike medicines that the federal Food and

Drug Administration (FDA) requires to be safe and effective, marijuana is unregulated, non-standardized, and not proven to be either safe or effective. Furthermore, because medical marijuana is not regulated, dosage is inconsistent and purity is unknown.

We are very sympathetic to anyone truly suffering from debilitating disease who is unable to obtain relief from traditional forms of treatment or medication. Therefore we will set forth a ten-point proposal that will permit those who possibly will benefit from marijuana use to obtain *prescription* marijuana, while obviating the fraud that characterizes most state-authorized medical marijuana programs.

Knowing what we know about marijuana today, and all the attendant problems that come with it, including many worse than those caused by tobacco (impairments of the brain, for example), we find it incredible that the move to legalize marijuana has become so mainstream. Indeed, beyond legalizing it for medical use (as twenty-three states and the District of Columbia have done), four states—Colorado, Washington, Oregon, and Alaska—have fully legalized the drug for recreational use, that is, any use whatsoever. The residents of the District of Columbia also voted to legalize recreational use. This makes us the first country in the world to have actually legalized marijuana, followed only recently by Uruguay.[2]

One final point: while there are dangerous substances that are legal in America (like tobacco and alcohol), we would be very ill-advised to add one more dangerous product (marijuana) to the list of things Americans should freely be able to obtain and use. We can add to the menu of dangerous substances available to our citizens, or we can draw a line and admit we are surfeited with the problems that already exist.

In fact, adding marijuana to the list of legal products will do little if anything to diminish the dangers or use of alcohol and tobacco; it will instead create yet more social and economic chaos. America does not need more of that. When a political leader known for liberal viewpoints voices objections to legalized marijuana, we know that this problem transcends party platforms because it is detrimental to our nation. As California Governor Jerry Brown recently said, "And all of a sudden, if there's advertising and legitimacy, how many people can get stoned and still have a great state or a great nation? The world's pretty dangerous, very competitive. I think we need to stay alert, if not twenty-four hours a day, more than some of the potheads might be able to put together."[3] Governor Brown is, of course, right to be talking about marijuana in the context of making Americans less productive in an increasingly competitive world. But that is merely one argument against legalization. There are many far more important.

The truths we will explain in this book:

- Marijuana is not safe.
- Marijuana is, except in a very few cases, not medicinal.
- Other countries that have experimented with decriminalization and tolerance are now trying to reverse such experiments.
- Already, American localities that have experimented with liberalization of marijuana laws are regretting it.
- There is no logical argument on behalf of states' rights to decide for themselves how to regulate marijuana, and it is not a fundamental right.

- Marijuana can be addictive.
- Marijuana use can be a gateway to other drug abuse.
- Marijuana is particularly harmful to, and addictive for, teenagers.
- And yes, we can reduce use and abuse of dangerous substances in America, just as we have before.

In the following pages we will lay out these positions and arguments, and take on the arguments on behalf of legalization that have influenced so many of our fellow citizens, but that we think are simply wrong. We believe the momentum toward legalization of marijuana can be stopped. It will require greater public awareness of the dramatic increase in the THC potency of present-day marijuana, and of the growing body of scientific evidence of the tremendous harm marijuana use can do to our health and our country. We hope this book will stimulate and contribute to that education effort.

Chapter 1

Marijuana Use Is Not Safe or Harmless. On the Contrary, It Is Dangerous.

Note to reader—I (Bill Bennett) have the privilege of hosting a national talk show and over time I have collected narratives and stories e-mailed to me by my listeners. We share some of them with you throughout the book, as we think they are narratives too many people do not hear, but that many of us will recognize as all too familiar. I begin with an e-mail from Greg in MI.

Dear Bill:

Please note when my son was 15 years old and sneaking marijuana I knew the destructive behavior and chaos that would ensue. My son is now 27 years old and a hopeless heroin addict living on the streets when he is not in prison. I have prayed and tried everything humanly possible at the cost of utter destruction of my family. Anyone that believes marijuana is harmless is like inviting your wife to have a boyfriend and believing things will be better in your marriage. Common sense is simple.

I t has become nearly commonplace to say and think that marijuana is not dangerous. After all, many of today's parents and grandparents smoked at least a little when they were younger. It is often no longer even called marijuana, but instead "medical marijuana," giving it a gloss of safety—something therapeutic, used for health. One often hears that marijuana is safer than alcohol, a fully legal substance found in almost every home. Indeed, the President of the United States recently made that claim in exactly those words in an interview with David Remnick of the *New Yorker*: "I don't think it is more dangerous than alcohol,"[1] President Obama said. This statement came after he first said that marijuana is "not very different from the cigarettes that I smoked as a young person up through a big chunk of my adult life."[2]

This is a sea change from just three presidential administrations ago, when President George H. W. Bush spoke directly to the nation about drug use—several times—saying such things as "Victory— victory over drugs—is our cause, a just cause. And with your help, we are going to win."[3] To our knowledge, President Obama— unlike his predecessors (both Republican and Democrat)—has given no speech on the issue of drug use and abuse during his presidency.

When the President of the United States says that marijuana is much like or less dangerous than alcohol—something most children see their parents drink—and likens it to tobacco cigarettes (which are used by 20 percent of the population), it becomes obvious that marijuana has lost its stigma. We understand why people would think it is not so bad. This motivates us to refute these claims.

Such statements about the innocence or benign nature of marijuana are not confined to Democrats such as President Obama. Republican Governor Bobby Jindal (R-LA) has come out in favor of legalizing "medical marijuana." US Senator Rand Paul (R-KY) has spoken out in favor of decriminalizing marijuana and protecting states that adopt "medical marijuana" laws. The nation's largest conservative conference—the Conservative Political Action Conference, or CPAC—is overwhelmingly populated by those opposed to marijuana's prohibition. Indeed, some prominent voices in the conservative movement and Republican Party are supporters of legalization.

The Risks That Are Being Ignored

The ancient Greeks believed that societies' views were often shaped by the leadership of their regime. If this is true, even in part, we can see why public opinion has moved the way it has, toward de-stigmatization and legalization. Should we not be asking, is marijuana as innocent as these and other leaders say? Enter this query into a search engine: "Marijuana teen brain." As of this writing, this is but a small sampling of what we found:

Marijuana May Hurt the Developing Teen Brain

Heavy Marijuana Use Alters Teenage Brain Structure

Marijuana: Why It's Still a Big Deal If Your Teen Smokes Pot

Perception of Marijuana as a "Safe Drug" Is Scientifically Inaccurate

Teen Pot Use Could Hurt Brain and Memory, New Research Suggests

Marijuana Use Linked to Concerning Brain Changes in Teens

Teen Marijuana Use Linked to Lower IQ in Later Life

Study Says Smoking Marijuana Worse for Lungs Than Cigarettes

Pot Increases Heart Attack Risks

Teenagers Who Smoke Cannabis Damage Their Brains for Life

Smoking Marijuana as Teen May Have Lasting Brain Effects[4]

These stories come from a wide variety of sources, including NPR, *Psychology Today,* Science Daily, NBC, CBS, and the *Daily Mail* of London. A sampling of these stories' researchers and sources? The brain imaging and neuropsychology lab at the University of Wisconsin–Milwaukee, Northwestern University Feinberg School of Medicine, the University of Montreal, New York's Icahn School of Medicine at Mount Sinai, the National Academy of Sciences, Boston's Beth Israel Deaconess Medical Center and Harvard Medical School, and the University of Maryland School of Medicine.

Now perform one other Internet search for us: "marijuana psychosis." Again, a modest sampling of what came up with the search engine we used:

The Cannabis-Psychosis Link
Marijuana May Both Trigger and Suppress Psychosis
How Marijuana May Drive the Brain into Psychosis
Prolonged Cannabis Use Linked to Psychosis
Marijuana Use Linked to Risk of Psychotic Symptoms
Teens Who Smoke Pot at Risk for Later Schizophrenia, Psychosis
Marijuana Use Precedes Psychosis[5]

Some of the sources include *Psychiatric Times*, *Time* magazine, LiveScience, Medical News Today, WebMD, and Reuters, and they are based on studies and analysis from such esteemed entities as the Department of Psychosis at King's College London; the Queensland Brain Institute, University of Queensland, Australia; the South Limburg Mental Health Research and Teaching Network of Maastricht University Medical Centre; Children's National Medical Center in Washington, D.C.; Harvard Medical School; the University of Wisconsin; Duke University; Northwestern University; University of Montreal; New York's Icahn School of Medicine at Mount Sinai; Oxford University Press's *Schizophrenia Bulletin*; the *New England Journal of Medicine*; the University of Maryland; the *Journal of Neuropsychopharmacology*; the Imperial College London; University College London; the *Journal of Psychoactive Drugs*; and the *Archives of General Psychiatry*, to list a sampling.

Any number of reasons have been used to justify legalization. Some people simply do not know of the current research on marijuana use or marijuana potency. But even dismissing the long-lasting and permanent serious health effects, if brain, lung, and heart function are not a worry for some, what of Governor Jerry Brown's point: decreased motivation and ambition? Do our students today—from elementary and secondary schools to colleges and universities—have the motivation and ambition, never mind health and brain power, to establish themselves, participate, and contribute to the increasingly competitive economy? Is there a single economist or corporate leader today who looks at the next generation's work ethic, schooling, and brainpower and sees no problem? Is this not the reason so many argue for more funding for early childhood education programs, as well as more money for our schools generally?

The science is in on this, making every dollar spent on improving our children's education a waste when it is countered by marijuana use. To wit: "The stereotype of pot smokers as lackadaisical loafers is supported by new research: People who smoke marijuana regularly over long periods of time tend to produce less of a chemical in the brain that is linked to motivation."[6] The study, out of one of Great Britain's finest schools of medicine, reveals what was self-evident. Nevertheless, here's the science: "Long-term cannabis users tended to produce less dopamine, a 'feel good' chemical in the brain that plays an important role in motivation and reward-driven behavior." This effect on dopamine levels will have other consequences for marijuana users as well—changing the developing brain in its pleasure reception and transmission. It is this effect that leads marijuana users to higher doses, higher concentrations of

THC, and other, harder, drugs. Similarly, it leads marijuana users to an ignorance of their self-destruction. As psychiatrist Robert DuPont, the president of the Institute for Behavior and Health, has written:

The fact that marijuana does not cause a hangover the way alcohol commonly does after heavy use is not an advantage at all. Marijuana stays in the brain for a long time so that the brain is still experiencing the effects from pot smoking days after the drug use has stopped, in contrast to alcohol use...

Unlike cocaine, which often brings users to their knees, marijuana claims its victims in a slower and more cruel fashion. It robs many of them of their desire to grow and improve, often making heavy users settle for what is left over in life...

Marijuana makes its users lose their purpose and their will, as well as their memory and motivation. Marijuana smokers do not often come into treatment for their addiction simply because neither they nor those around them can differentiate their true selves from the effects of their drug use. They commonly just sink lower and lower in their performance and in their goals in life as their pot smoking continues. Their hopes and lives literally go up in marijuana smoke.[7]

Drug Use and Stigmatization

We will delve more deeply into what these studies mean, but as a first question: has anyone ever alleged anything like the foregoing with tobacco use? Yet society has successfully and rightly stigmatized tobacco use for both health and cosmetic reasons. Indeed, the idea that we, as a society, cannot stop the consumption of addictive substances or, as it is often more crudely put, "win the war on drugs," is belied by our experience with tobacco cigarettes. Since the mid-1970s, cigarette smoking in America has declined by more than half, from about 43 percent of Americans admitting to smoking (38 percent in 1983) to just under 20 percent today.[8]

How did we accomplish this? We did it through a culture of education, promulgating the health risks, increasing the price of cigarettes, cracking down on sales to minors, and stigmatizing tobacco use. In fact, noting a slowing decrease of smoking rates among teenagers, a recent piece in *Time* magazine listed the reasons for this: "fewer anti-smoking ads," cigars' becoming less expensive, a lack of graphic labels on cigarette packages as in other countries, and new marketing efforts for tobacco with "enticing flavors."[9]

It is clear how we got illicit drug use down in the early 1990s, and how and why we have seen it rise again since—having let up on the cultural messages, we no longer talk or teach about it; and we have abandoned fighting the nonsense about it. But why the disconnect between tobacco and marijuana? Why is one stigmatized now and the other seen as benign? People now generally understand that the best way to prevent tobacco use is to never start. The first two sentences of the *Time* magazine story: "The surest way to stop smoking tobacco? Never start." One can replace "tobacco" with "marijuana" or "drugs" throughout the story and perceive why teen use of marijuana has been on the increase: "Fewer anti-smoking ads." "Lower prices." "Enticing flavors." At every point there is a drug analogue. It is increasingly enigmatic to us why so many care about tobacco use, which harms the lungs, but are so blasé—or worse, even encouraging—about marijuana use, which harms the lungs *and* the brain, sometimes even permanently.

We simply do not now see or hear ads about marijuana the way we do tobacco. In Arizona in the 1990s, for example, a series of anti-cigarette ads ran. The message: "Cigarette Smoking: tumor-causing, teeth-staining, smelly, puking habit." Health officials are quoted as stating that smoking rates dropped over 20 percent in the 1990s as a result of those ads.[10] As one teen who saw the ad put it, "Those ads are gross and it makes me think smoking isn't for me."[11] Today there are no messages like that regarding marijuana use. In fact, it is quite the opposite; use is encouraged. The result is that marijuana use is up. According to one recent study by Rand, marijuana use has increased more than 30 percent between 2006 and 2010, and today more teens are smoking marijuana than tobacco cigarettes, 23 percent marijuana to 18 percent tobacco.[12]

We have turned what was once stigmatized into so-called medicine, regarding marijuana not as something dangerous, but as actually therapeutic or helpful. Today, twenty-three states plus the District of Columbia provide for and allow "medical marijuana" use. A medical marijuana proposition was defeated in Florida in November 2014. However, in Oregon, Alaska, and the

District of Columbia, voters in 2014 approved propositions legalizing recreational marijuana, as was passed in the states of Washington and Colorado in 2012. This snowball is gaining momentum
as it rolls downhill: earlier in 2014, the California Democratic Party
"voted to support legalizing, taxing and regulating marijuana for
all uses—medicinal, recreational and industrial."[13] The largest
political party in the most populous state in the country is now on
record as officially in favor of legalizing marijuana.

The Cultural Message

Beyond the politics, what of the culture? *Redbook* magazine recently
did a story on how more and more parents are smoking marijuana:
"I'm a Parent Who Smokes Pot"—"That's the wild health confes-
sion REDBOOK heard from a surprising number of moms. They
claim it's a harmless, even helpful, habit. Are they right... or totally
high?" The story opens this way:

> Alice, a 37-year-old mom in Madison, WI, made a recent walk
> with her two daughters more fun by naming the neighborhood
> wildlife, starting with Squirrely Squirrelson and his cousin,
> Squirrelster McSquirrelstein. "My 4-year-old cracked up, and
> that made my 2-year-old dissolve into giggles," remembers
> Alice. "My kids demanded that I name every animal in sight,
> and I encouraged them to think of their own names too." Cute
> story, right? Is it less cute if I tell you that Mom was a little bit
> stoned?[14]

Alice goes on to say,

> …she does it for fun or to chill out, and, occasionally, to get into what she calls the "kid zone." "If I had been perfectly sober, I would have just taken a walk, thinking about what I needed to do next," Alice says. "I probably wouldn't have been all that engaged with my kids. But the stoned mama that I was that day made fun out of the mundane."[15]

As the story reports, more and more parents are doing this, because "marijuana can be medicinal, and some parents are using it like a quick-fix antidepressant or anti-anxiety medication." The reporter even tells us, "Marijuana is notably less toxic and addictive than alcohol or cigarettes, but you can still get hooked."[16]

More and more parents are actually suggesting their children smoke marijuana as opposed to taking other substances (as if responsible parenting wouldn't dictate saying no to all harmful substances). As one "mommy blog" quotes, in a post that was titled, "Pot Parents: Smoking Better Than Drinking," more and more moms "prefer" their children choose the lesser of two evils. "Things have gotten so skewed. People look at pot like it's the bogeyman. It's not going to kill you; alcohol can kill you," said Diane, one of the moms interviewed.[17]

Between the new parent-pot chic and the efforts to medicalize and legalize marijuana for recreational use, we can better come to understand the de-stigmatization that has taken place. We should be no less understanding of what it has led to: according to an article citing the most recent National Institutes of Health/National Institute on Drug Abuse (NIDA) report on attitudes toward marijuana, "just 39.5 percent of high school seniors view regular marijuana use as harmful. That's down from 2012's rate of 44.1 percent, and considerably lower than rates from the past two decades." According to the article, the study indicates:

> Young people are showing less disapproval of marijuana use and decreased perception that marijuana is dangerous...The growing perception of marijuana as a safe drug may reflect recent public discussions over medical marijuana and movements to legalize the drug for adult recreational use in some states.[18]

Or, as one fourteen-year veteran of the Salt Lake City Police Department more directly put it:

> You talk to the kids and with everything that's going on with it being legalized in Colorado and comments being made that it's just not that bad for you, the kids are taking it one step further and they're telling me, "It's just an herb. It's OK. In fact, it's used for medical purposes, it's not bad for you. It's good for you." And that's the belief that our kids are getting.[19]

Marijuana Harms the Lungs

So, let's get to it: just how dangerous is marijuana? Is it less harmful than tobacco or alcohol? Can it be medicinal? Let us start with the respiratory system. According to NIDA:

Marijuana smoke is an irritant to the lungs, and frequent marijuana smokers can have many of the same respiratory problems experienced by tobacco smokers, such as daily cough and phlegm production, more frequent acute chest illness, and a heightened risk of lung infections. One study found that people who smoke marijuana frequently but do not smoke tobacco have more health problems and miss more days of work than those who don't smoke marijuana, mainly because of respiratory illnesses.[20]

According to the American Lung Association:

There are 33 cancer-causing chemicals contained in marijuana. Marijuana smoke also deposits tar into the lungs. In fact, when equal amounts of marijuana and tobacco are smoked, marijuana deposits four times as much tar into the lungs. This is because marijuana joints are un-filtered and often more deeply inhaled than cigarettes.

Marijuana smoke is also an irritant to the lungs, and frequent marijuana smokers can have many of the same respiratory problems experienced by people who smoke tobacco.[21]

It is true, however, that one can find studies stating marijuana smoking is less harmful than tobacco cigarette smoking or even that moderate marijuana smoking does not contribute to lung impairment. There is, nonetheless, a problem with those studies. As

Dr. Eric Vallieres, director of thoracic surgery at the Swedish Medical Center in Seattle, has put it:

> These studies, however, are limited by the fact that many marijuana smokers are also cigarette smokers, that some users mix tobacco and marijuana in their joint, and that the illegality of marijuana use may have influenced the willingness of participants to give honest answers regarding their use of marijuana, affecting the validity of the data used in these studies.[22]

Moreover, Dr. Vallieres writes:

> Laboratory work has demonstrated the occurrence of tissue, cellular and molecular pre-cancerous changes in the airways and lungs of cannabis users that are strikingly similar to those seen in cigarette smokers. Similarly, the carcinogenic effects of cannabis smoke have been demonstrated in both human and animal models: marijuana smoke contains 50 to 70% more carcinogenic hydrocarbons than tobacco smoke. Additional factors that may contribute to the carcinogenic potential of marijuana smoke are the tendency for marijuana to burn at a higher temperature and that marijuana smoke is typically inhaled deeper and held longer than tobacco smoke (two factors that promote prolonged contact duration of potential carcinogens on the lung lining).
>
> Some argue that one or two joints per day of exposure to these carcinogens does not even come close to the 1–2 packs

per day contact a cigarette smoker experiences. While this may mathematically make sense, the fact is that we do not know of a safe level for such exposures.[23]

Beyond the studies showing the connection between marijuana use and lung damage, one might want to step back for one moment and ask, is it even possible that smoking and inhaling a product, a carcinogen, would not have a negative effect on the pulmonary system? It belies common sense.

Marijuana's Negative Impact on the Adolescent Brain

We highlighted a series of stories about marijuana and the brain earlier. Now let us be more specific. Here is how marijuana works on the teen and young adult brain. The brain is in development through a person's early to mid-twenties. Introducing marijuana into the brain during this time can actually change its normal and natural development. As Joe Califano of the National Center on Addiction and Substance Abuse at Columbia University puts it in his book *How to Raise a Drug-Free Kid*, "Whatever the substance, brains of repeat drug users are 'rewired,' becoming predisposed to cravings...As a result, to increase dopamine levels and experience resulting pleasure, the addict needs to use drugs. And the more frequently and longer an addict uses drugs, the more drugs he or she needs to create the high."[24] This is the definition of a vicious cycle.

Put another way, marijuana affects receptors in the brain that are responsible for everything from memory to pleasure response. As noted on *Science Daily*, the Society of Nuclear Medicine and Molecular Imaging found, "abuse of the drug led to a decreased number of cannabinoid CB1 receptors, which are involved in not just pleasure, appetite and pain tolerance but a host of other psychological and physiological functions of the body."[25]

Consider the teen brain and what marijuana, the drug most commonly abused by teens, does. As a *Psychology Today* article points out, based on a recent study:

> Teenagers who use marijuana regularly are at greater risk for long-term brain damage and declines in both IQ and cognitive functioning years later. Daily cannabis use is on the rise among adolescents who are now smoking marijuana at younger ages than ever before, many of them on a daily basis. This rise in marijuana use is caused in part because most teenagers do not believe that smoking marijuana is harmful to their health.[26]

Why is this? In part, to quote from a study from the Massachusetts Chapter of the American Academy of Pediatrics:

> During the first decade of life, brain growth occurs mainly in the gray matter (neurons and dendrites) and during the second and third decades, it occurs primarily in the white matter (connectivity). Exposure to neurotoxins during the brain's developmental period can permanently alter the brain's structure and function.[27]

That is what marijuana does to the teen brain: it alters the structure and function. Because of a vicious cycle that numbs the reward and pleasure responses in the brain, more and more is required to obtain such pleasure—or such a high. This is but one reason marijuana users are much more likely to try harder drugs than those who never initiate marijuana use. With all the challenges our adolescents face today, negatively altering their brain structures and functions is destructive to both individuals and society.

The Increased Risk Posed by Today's Turbo Marijuana

Why do so many parents and grandparents, who may not be familiar with this new research and literature, still think marijuana is not worse than cigarettes or is mostly harmless? We believe they are unaware of the prevalence and the strength of marijuana today. There is much more marijuana use now than there was a generation or two ago, and, what's worse, the substance itself is far more powerful than the marijuana society got used to in the late 1960s and throughout the 1970s. What about that seemingly innocent pot that we see being smoked in historical footage from Woodstock? It is no longer innocent: marijuana is more potent than at any time since scientific analysis of the drug began in the 1970s. The average amount of THC in marijuana today, the primary psychoactive ingredient in the drug, is about 9.6 to 13 percent, more than double the potency of marijuana in 1983, which was more than double what it was the decade before. We also are seeing THC levels skyrocket in some samples being marketed and used. The Cannabis Cup (an annual competition sponsored by *High Times* magazine) boasts strains containing 25 percent THC, and the Marijuana Potency Project at the University of Mississippi has found levels of THC as high as 37 percent. That is a growth of a psychoactive ingredient from 3 and 4 percent a few decades ago to close to 40 percent.[28] The full effects of these strains on the brain are yet unknown, even as they are becoming more and more popular. But we do know the effects are not salutary; in fact, we know they are dangerous.

Dear Bill:

My husband and I are 67 and 69. Last year we went to a Steely Dan concert and our neighbor (36 yrs old) gave us some marijuana and with a smile said "be careful." We hadn't smoked pot for 30 or more years and we thought "why not?" and we blew off his warning saying, "We know, we've smoked pot before." Off we went and with true teenage abandon we took two puffs each in our car in a casino parking garage. We looked at each other and agreed...we didn't feel anything. A few minutes later we attempted to step out of our SUV and almost fell. It came on so fast and so strong. We had to navigate an elevator, walk through the casino, out to the street and two blocks to where the concert was being held. We were having to focus 100% on the act of walking. The doors to the venue weren't open and we stood up against the building, away from people just waiting to be able to get to our seats and ride it out. My husband wanted to slide down the wall and sit on the sidewalk but he was afraid he wouldn't be able to get up...Everything visual and auditory was exaggerated and distorted. This new marijuana is waaaaaaay beyond simple medical use for pain. It lasted about six hours with the first three hours being at its strongest. There is no way we could have or would have driven the first three hours. Sit in a classroom and learn, impossible. Sit at the dinner table with your family and enjoy a conversation, impossible. This is not a couple of beers. This is not a couple of martinis. This is being drugged.

Nancy in NV

Odd to us is the idea that when other legal products have their addictive or psychoactive ingredient jacked up—think high-alcohol malt beer or higher nicotine contents in cigarettes—the culture usually pushes back. The tobacco companies now actually try to market lower-nicotine cigarettes or "lights." However, when it comes to marijuana, the rules are different. The ingredient most active on the brain, THC—which has far worse consequences to the brain than tobacco or nicotine—is increasing year after year, and yet there are "cups" or awards given to those manufacturers who produce the new strains. The move by the culture, as with public opinion, is to continue on the path toward more legalization and availability, and higher THC rates.

Not Just Adolescent Brains Are Injured

Although research regarding the impact of the higher levels of THC on the brain is ongoing, we have some evidence already:

> "There's an increase in psych admissions," says Dr. Stuart Gitlow, a psychiatrist who estimates that upwards of 1 in 100 people using high-THC marijuana experience psychotic symptoms. As president of the American Society of Addiction Medicine, Gitlow also worries about the long-term impact.
>
> "If you look at marijuana, the intensity has changed. So I would expect it to have a somewhat higher addictive potential."
>
> Dr. Christian Thurstone, who runs an addiction treatment center in Denver, agrees that there is a trend toward heavier use. He's seen steadily higher levels of THC metabolites in clients' urine tests when they enter his program. "It's more difficult to get kids clean," Thurstone says, "because they come in less motivated for treatment, and more addicted."[29]

There is a concern that the drive for more legalization and availability will "dumb down" America and Americans. The science on marijuana use and its effects on intelligence supports this. Take this headline from WebMD last year: "Cannabis Use in Teens Linked to Irreparable Drop in IQ."[30] Or this headline from the *New York Times*: "Early Marijuana Use Linked to IQ Loss."[31] Now take the opening line from the first story: "Cannabis users who start smoking the drug as adolescents show an irreparable decline in IQ, with more persistent use linked to a greater decline, new research shows." The last line of the story should frighten: "Cessation of cannabis did not restore IQ among teen-onset cannabis users." Even tobacco smokers can restore lung function years after cessation of smoking. The brain, though, is not the lungs, and marijuana brain damage can be permanent. It can also lead to all manner of academic problems—including dropping out of school entirely—and job prospect limitations. After all, an eight-point drop in IQ can mean the difference between someone being "very gifted" and "gifted," or "gifted" and "superior," or "superior" and "high average," or "high average" and "average," or "average" and "low average," or "low average" and "borderline impaired," or "borderline impaired" and worse.[32]

While the study on marijuana and IQ—from Duke University—has been subjected to criticism and challenges, as is typical of almost every study on every issue, the authors have defended it. Dr. Nora Volkow, the director of NIDA, has said of the study:

The message inherent in these and in multiple supporting studies is clear. Regular marijuana use in adolescence is known to be part of a cluster of behaviors that can produce enduring detrimental effects and alter the trajectory of a young person's life—thwarting his or her potential. Beyond potentially lowering IQ, teen marijuana use is linked to school dropout, other drug use, mental health problems, etc. . . . regular marijuana use stands to jeopardize a young person's chances of success—in school and in life.[33]

So the question now presents itself, what are the chances these studies are right? One hundred percent? Fifty percent? Twenty-five percent? Let us hypothesize severe skepticism and say, for argument's sake, all these studies have a 5 percent chance of being right—a 5 percent chance of showing that teen marijuana use *can* lead to lower IQ, a 5 percent chance that teen marijuana use *may* lead to psychosis in *some* users, a 5 percent chance that teen marijuana use *could* lead to other mental health problems. Now ask yourself this: if a doctor prescribed you a medicine and said, "There's a small risk, maybe five percent, that this drug can lead to a lower IQ or psychosis," would you ever even consider taking it or giving it to your teenager? Such a drug certainly would not pass FDA muster and the manufacturer of such a drug would be subject to the kind of lawsuit that would put it out of business.

Think about the drug Vioxx for a moment. It was known as a "blockbuster" pain and arthritis medication. However, in 2004 it was pulled off the shelves and its manufacturer was subject to all manner of litigation when it was discovered 3.5 percent of its users suffered heart attacks as opposed to 1.9 percent taking a placebo.[34] Those a little older may remember the drug thalidomide. Some called it a "miracle drug" because of its sedative and anti-nausea properties. Thalidomide was banned in America in the early 1960s (it is now being used again for populations not at risk) after it was noted that some ten thousand babies born *worldwide* had suffered birth defects from it, about 10 percent of the thalidomide-using population.[35] The point is this: when there is a risk—3 percent, higher, lower—of a drug or substance negatively affecting our or our children's health, we as a society have been rigorous about reducing the risk or pulling that product from the market. We have banned the use of drugs with far lower chances of damage than we see in all the studies coming out about the dangerous side effects of marijuana.

With marijuana we have inexplicably suspended all the normal rules of reasoning and knowledge.

The Marijuana Paradox

It is perplexing that we are so in favor of marijuana when there are ever-growing public policy debates about mandating earlier education for our youth, for example, mandatory federally subsidized preschool. The goal is to give our children a better head start and increase their chances of success in life with better education and effective brain power. We have health care policy debates— especially about funding and reach—to ensure the health of our youth. Indeed, a large part of the Affordable Care Act was its mandate of health care coverage not only for children, but also for teens and young adults. This country rightly cares about and spends a lot of money on child health and education. Introducing a once-illegal substance into the sphere (brains and lungs) of our youth is not only societal cognitive dissonance, it is public policy malpractice. In 2014 Elliott Kaye was President Obama's nominee to chair the Consumer Product Safety Commission.[36] He had served as its executive director until his nomination to that role. Up to his nomination, his best-known efforts had been to ensure better safety standards for football helmets, from the NFL down to young players in amateur sports. Mr. Kaye won bipartisan praise for these efforts and said that, if confirmed, "brain safety" will be his top priority. The hearing on his confirmation was lauded in the press as one of refreshing bipartisan agreement.[37]

Here is the disconnect. From early childhood to the NFL (where players are actually adults and know the risks), there are multiple efforts to protect brains. We endeavor to help develop and enrich them at as early an age as possible; other efforts are geared toward protecting them physically, in everything from car safety to football safety. Yet here we have a drug, legalized by four states, called medicine in many others, and being propagated as harmless (at worst) and therapeutic (at best), when every serious study of the effects of marijuana on the teen brain says there is at least *some* cause for concern.

Why do we focus on the teen brain? For a very simple reason— most drug users, over 90 percent of them, including marijuana users, started using drugs in their adolescent years. In fact, if one abstains from substance abuse up until the age of twenty-one, the chances one will ever have a substance abuse problem are next to zero. As we will show in the next chapter, efforts to medicalize and legalize marijuana for adults, that is, to make marijuana available for people only over the age of eighteen or twenty-one, have failed. How many of you know or know of someone under the age of twenty-one who has been able to drink alcohol, how many under the age of eighteen who has been able to buy cigarettes? Those legal products are, after all, banned from being sold to people under twenty-one and eighteen, respectively. Yet teen use of alcohol and tobacco is through the roof. Nearly ten million underage people currently use alcohol, and nearly six million of them are binge drinkers.[38] Nearly 25 percent of high school students use tobacco products today.[39] Substance abuse and addiction generally begin before age twenty-one. As Dr. Nora Volkow from NIDA puts it, "There is no question that marijuana can be addictive; that argument is over. The most important thing right now is to understand the vulnerability of young developing brains to these increased concentrations of cannabis."[40]

Earlier we asked you to perform an Internet search for "marijuana" and "psychosis," and provided a sampling of headlines. Here are a few more:

Cannabis May Increase Stroke Risk

Legalizing of Marijuana Raises Health Concerns

Scientists Warn of Cannabis Link to Heart Attacks

Wake-up Call for Teen Pot Smokers; Study Links Cannabis Use with Psychosis

Marijuana Use Linked to Psychotic Symptoms in Teenagers

A Risk Gene for Cannabis Psychosis

The Cannabis-Psychosis Link

Marijuana Linked to Psychosis in Teens

Doctors: Marijuana Triggers Psychosis

You get the point. Summarizing her work, Dr. Sion Kim Harris, director of the Survey Research Methods Core of the Clinical Research Program of the Boston Children's Hospital, puts it this way: "Besides the evidence showing that marijuana affects memory and cognitive performance, there is a growing body of evidence suggesting that marijuana may increase risk for mental illness."[41] To wit: "Regular marijuana use during adolescence [has been] found to increase risk 2 to 5 times of developing psychosis, schizophrenia, anxiety, and depression in adulthood."[42] A recent report by the Northwestern University School of Medicine demonstrated that if someone has a family history of schizophrenia, that person increases his or her risk of developing schizophrenia by regularly using marijuana.[43]

Marijuana's Short-Term Impact on Judgment, Coordination, and Motor Skills

Beyond what marijuana can do to the brain in the long run—as with cigarette smoking and lung cancer or COPD—there is new evidence on driving impairment: "Recent national statistics show that, among fatally injured drivers who were randomly selected for drug testing (excluding tobacco, alcohol, and medications administered after the crash), more and more are testing positive for marijuana. In 2009, the rate of positive tests had increased to one in three. Among positive tests, marijuana was the most common drug found."[44] Dennis Prager has analyzed this point best, distinguishing between the effects of marijuana and cigarettes on the brain: would you rather get in an airplane where the pilot had just smoked a cigarette or a joint? Or just keep it to driving cars: as Dr. Marilyn A. Huestis of NIDA has found, "several researchers, working independently of one another, have come up with the same estimate: a twofold increase in the risk of an [automobile] accident if there is any measurable amount of THC in the bloodstream."[45] Does any parent in America think it a good idea to give car keys to a sixteen-year-old who uses a product that increases twofold the chance of an automobile accident?

Negative Consequences for the Heart

Most of this chapter has discussed current studies detailing marijuana's effects on the brain and lungs. But what of the heart? We know the following:

> Marijuana also raises heart rate by 20–100 percent shortly after smoking; this effect can last up to 3 hours. In one study, it was estimated that marijuana users have a 4.8-fold increase in the risk of heart attack in the first hour after smoking the drug.[46]

It seems that almost every couple of months, another study comes out on the dangers of marijuana. No studies conclude that it is benign. This recent headline from the *Los Angeles Times* is illustrative: "Potential for heart attack, stroke risk seen with marijuana use." Here is a précis of that article:

> Over a five-year period, a government-mandated tracking system in France showed that physicians in that country treated

1,979 patients for serious health problems associated with the use of marijuana, and nearly 2% of those encounters were with patients suffering from cardiovascular problems, including heart attack, cardiac arrhythmia and stroke, and circulation problems in the arms and legs. In roughly a quarter of those cases, the study found, the patient died.

In the United States, when young and otherwise healthy patients show up in emergency departments with symptoms of heart attack, stroke, cardiomyopathy and cardiac arrhythmia, physicians have frequently noted in case reports that these unusual patients are regular marijuana users...

"There is now compelling evidence on the growing risk of marijuana-associated adverse cardiovascular effects, especially in young people," said Emilie Jouanjus, lead author of the French study, which was also published in the *Journal of the American Heart Assn.* That evidence, Jouanjus added, should prompt cardiologists to consider marijuana use a potential cause of cardiovascular disease in patients they see.[47]

Another major study on the dangers of marijuana was released in October 2014 by Dr. Wayne Hall of the University of Queensland, published in the journal *Addiction.* The study was described in the media as "a sweeping new review of 20 years of research into the recreational use of marijuana."[48] Here are some of the major findings from the study's abstract: "Research in the past 20 years has shown that driving while cannabis-impaired approximately doubles car crash risk and that around one in 10 regular cannabis users develop dependence. Regular cannabis use in adolescence approximately doubles the risks of early school-leaving and of cognitive impairment and psychoses in adulthood." The abstract's conclusion: "The epidemiological literature in the past 20 years shows that cannabis use increases the risk of accidents and can produce dependence, and that there are consistent associations between regular cannabis use and poor psychosocial outcomes and mental health in adulthood."[49]

Can all these studies be wrong? What is the Pascal's wager here? Assume we are wrong and marijuana is harmless (a big assumption given all the scientific research that is coming in). Do we need it? Is there any anecdotal evidence at all that it is good for our teens? Turning the wager around: what if all or most or even just some of these studies are right? Are we not about to unleash a new flood of health problems on society with the growing effort to normalize and legalize marijuana?

The culture has convinced itself marijuana is harmless or that the risks to health are worth taking for the benefit of the therapy... or the high. As more and more evidence mounts that marijuana is dangerous, especially for the young, it is a shame so many are trying to make it widely available and legal. It is an assault on our youth and their brains. It is a foolish idea that, should it win the day, will reduce IQs and ambition, and make Americans mentally and physically sicker.

Chapter 2

What Is "Medical Marijuana"?

N early half the states in America, plus the District of Columbia, have legalized some form of marijuana use—mostly for "medicinal" purposes. Four states have fully legalized marijuana for "recreational" use. Rather than exhaustively analyze every state's experience with medical marijuana and what Washington and Colorado have done, we will instead examine some experiences in a few of these states.

A Wide Variety of State-Authorized Medical Marijuana Programs

Medical marijuana programs vary greatly among the various states that have legalized them. In Colorado and California, for example, thousands of neighborhood dispensaries sell marijuana to anyone with a medical marijuana identification card, which is very easily obtained. In New York, which legalized medical marijuana in 2014, the program is quite different. Only five private companies will be selected to open and operate four dispensaries each. There is a narrow list of eligibility requirements, and any doctor who prescribes marijuana to a patient who does not truly meet the criteria may be charged with a felony. Finally, patients may consume marijuana only through food, oils, pills, or vapors. Smoking marijuana is prohibited.[1] It is striking that Colorado has more than five hundred medical marijuana dispensaries with a population of 5.1 million people, while New York has authorized a total of twenty dispensaries with a population of 19.5 million people.

In California, medicinal marijuana was approved in 1996 by about 55 percent of the vote. In 2000, Colorado voters passed a referendum legalizing the use of medical marijuana with approximately 54 percent of the vote. Just to point out that this is not a red state/blue state issue, in 2010, Arizona voters approved their medical marijuana law with just over 50 percent of the vote. In November 2014, voters in Oregon, Alaska, and the District of Columbia voted in favor of outright, recreational legalization. Florida voters rejected a referendum initiative that would have permitted medical marijuana.

Not content with the idea of marijuana use for only medicinal purposes, four states have now gone on to fully legalize recreational use of the drug. This makes the United States only the second nation in the world with fully legalized marijuana use (Uruguay is the other). Not even the Netherlands, notorious as it is for its liberal cannabis

policies, formally legalized the sale or use of pot—it merely toler-
ates it with liberalized laws on enforcement.[2] Not so Washington
and Colorado, where possession is now, by law, legal. The voters in
Colorado enacted their recreational use law in 2012 with 55 percent
of the vote; the voters in Washington passed their law the same year,
with the same percentage.

The Federal Government Has Abdicated
Its Legal Responsibility

Keep in mind that none of this affects federal law and it is in direct
opposition to the federal Controlled Substances Act. Most of us
were taught in high school that under the US Constitution, federal
law is the supreme law of the land, and states may not violate federal law. Marijuana is allowed to play by a different standard, and
even the Obama administration and the Department of Justice have
said they will not enforce the federal law against the states that have
contravened federal law when it comes to marijuana. Those who
took history and civics classes also may remember such concepts
as nullification, and that the Civil War put the issue to rest: states
may not contravene federal law. Yet nearly half have, with little or
no legal consequence. Indeed, the Attorney General of the United
States has gone so far as to endorse the states' thumbing of their
noses at the federal law: "I think, so far, I'm cautiously optimistic," about the laws in Colorado and Washington, said Eric Holder.
"But as I indicated to both governors, we will be monitoring the
progress of those efforts and if we conclude that they are not being

done in an appropriate way, we reserve our rights to file lawsuits."[3] This statement is about two states' laws that contravene the federal law, which holds that the possession of any amount of marijuana is illegal. The states decided to go another way and the Attorney General is "optimistic." What message does this send to other states? To law enforcement? To children who used to be taught marijuana was illegal because it was dangerous? The US Attorney General has effectively said "not illegal" and "not so dangerous." Recall, too, that the President has compared smoking marijuana to smoking tobacco cigarettes, something children and others see being done all the time.

The federal/state conflict informs much of the political debate over marijuana, especially among libertarians on the right. Democrats and the left have not usually been the political precinct in favor of states' rights (but, again, marijuana changes all the usual rules). We will look at whether the federal laws are, indeed, right. However, for the moment, to answer the question about whether the federal laws are correct, what have been the consequences in California, Washington, Colorado, Arizona, and other states? Early though this experiment in legalization is, we already have some data—and it is not encouraging. On the contrary, it is bad.

"Medical Marijuana for All"—the Medical Marijuana Myth

Let us start with medical marijuana. Defining *medicine* through legislative fiat or popular referendum undermines the national drug approval system run by the FDA. The FDA has stringent technical and evidence-based standards that it uses to protect all Americans from dangerous, ineffective, or fraudulent drugs. It puts in place safeguards that include confirmed purity; validated production; tightly controlled manufacturing; known shelf life, microbiology, and efficacy and safety data per dose; documented side-effect profiles; and regular safety updates to keep the FDA apprised. While its approval system may not be perfect, it has shielded us from many unsafe and unacceptable drugs for decades.

As many in the media are wont to say—and many in the culture have adopted such language—one needs a doctor's prescription to obtain medical marijuana. This is simply untrue. No doctor in America can actually prescribe marijuana: it would violate the acceptable use of his Drug Enforcement Agency–authorized prescription drug pad. What the state laws require are not prescriptions, but recommendation notes or letters from a doctor (or a card issued by the state based on a letter from a doctor). The distinction is important as, again, the culture and children learn from the language that is being used: marijuana is simply not medicine a doctor can prescribe, no matter what it is called. It is not medicine to be found in any pharmacy. Additionally, never in the history of the FDA has there been an authorized form of medicine that is lit up and inhaled. There are doctors who are willing to write notes to patients who can go to dispensaries to buy marijuana cigarettes and brownies, or grow their own. Not pharmacies, but dispensaries and backyards—another important distinction. Unlike medicine, marijuana has no set or controlled dose or strength—that is left up to the users, dispensaries, and growers, many of whom compete for business based on the THC potency of their marijuana. In other words, there is a "race to the top" with dispensaries advertising or promoting higher and higher levels of THC in their product.

How easy is it to obtain such a note, letter, or card? Here's Will Wooton, a drug and alcohol counselor in Escondido, California:

"First it was almost unbelievable. It was just hard to imagine that you could easily obtain something that can be misused," Wooton said. "Most of the kids think it's a joke. In fact, they openly say it's a get out of jail free card. That is one of the nicknames around high school."

Wooton said he used to see one to two teenagers a month who used their medical marijuana card as a means to get high. Now he sees more than that every week.

Legally, you must be at least 18 years old to obtain a medical marijuana card, but FOX 5 wanted to find out what else was required, so we decided to follow Wooton's fellow counselor, Grant Glidewell, as he tried to get a card.

The first clinic we stopped at was in the North County… "The most common thing I hear from kids is that they go in and say they're anxious and can't sleep. I'm going to give that a shot and I'm pretty confident that will work," said Glidewell.

It did work. Less than an hour later, Glidewell walked out of the first clinic with a card to legally smoke pot.

"When I saw the doctor, he smiled and had looked over my questionnaire briefly. He said, 'You have two of three main symptoms we treat here,'" Glidewell said. "He then said that

I was going to love marijuana, that he and his wife smoked it and that I was going to have the best sleep of my life."[4]

Gone are the days when teenagers wanting to break the law and get high had to plan for days how they would obtain their weed. No more calling friends, and friends of friends, and negotiating prices at covert (often seedy) meeting places. Now, one hour, one pot card. What are the conditions needed to obtain a marijuana recommendation? In California and other states the list is rather long, ranging from cancer to chronic pain. But it can also include any "medical condition that limits the ability of the patient to conduct one or more major life activities."[5] Demand, of course, is high. Thus, so is supply. There seems to be an awful lot of chronic pain out there.

We mean no offense to those with serious illnesses—and we will address this issue further on—but they are an extremely small percentage among the many who are obtaining medical marijuana cards and notes. In Arizona, thirty-four thousand people had medical marijuana cards as of December 2012. *Arizona Republic* reporter Laurie Roberts says that "3.76 percent use marijuana to ease the symptoms of cancer. Another 1.53 percent suffer from glaucoma while 1.06 percent have AIDS. Meanwhile 89.8 percent—30,203 people—are seeking relief for 'severe and chronic pain.'" Only 13 percent of cardholders are over sixty; "nearly 73 percent of patients are men and the people most likely to seek relief from their pain are 18 to 30 years old." Roberts was in favor of the law—before she saw its effects, even its early effects. After the law passed and after seeing the numbers above, and the types of people lining up in front of the state's first dispensary—"not exactly glaucoma-stricken grannies," as she put it—she changed her mind, calling the law "a charade." Here is how she opened her column: "I was all set to go along with the charade. All the talk of patients, of care-givers and medicine. But the picture of the teen-age kid holding his skateboard as he came out of Arizona's first medical marijuana dispensary...Oh come on!"[6]

Other states show much the same, making one wonder why a recreational law need even be passed when there is a medicinal one. As Maricopa county attorney (aka the district attorney) Bill Montgomery put it, "There's not a single state with a medical marijuana act or anything similar that hasn't turned into a recreational use program."[7] In Colorado, for instance, severe pain is the reported condition for 94 percent of medical marijuana users. Three percent have cancer, 1 percent have HIV/AIDS. Seventy-four percent of the patients are male. In California, "fewer than 2 percent of [cardholders] have HIV, glaucoma, multiple sclerosis, or cancer."[8] What of the idea that only adults can use medical marijuana? Two hundred and forty-eight medical marijuana cards have been issued to children under the age of eighteen in Colorado.[9]

Medical Marijuana Finds Its Way to Children

Moreover, regardless of what legalizers have said about wanting a system whereby marijuana can be regulated and kept from children, even before Coloradans voted in legalized recreational use of marijuana, their medical marijuana was getting into the hands (and lungs, brains, and hearts) of children. As the *Denver Post* reported in the summer of 2012, "Nearly three-quarters of teens in two metro-area substance-abuse treatment programs said they have used medical marijuana bought or grown for someone else, according to a new study by researchers at the University of Colorado School of Medicine...In surveys conducted of the teens, researchers asked whether the teens had ever used somebody else's medical marijuana and, if so, how often. Seventy-four percent of the teens said they had, with a median frequency of 50 times."[10]

Note, too, for those who like to say marijuana is neither addictive nor harmful, these were teens in substance abuse programs, trying to get sober from marijuana use. In fact, nationwide, one-third of teenagers who live in states with medical marijuana laws get their pot from other people's "prescriptions."[11] Marijuana usage by twelve- to seventeen-year-olds is dramatically higher in states that have legalized marijuana.

Past Month Use by 12 to 17-Year-Olds Medical Marijuana States vs. Non-Medical Marijuana States

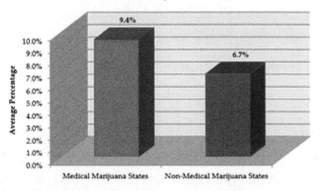

SOURCE: Data from SAMHSA.gov, National Survey on Drug Use and Health, 2013

Nationwide, over 70 percent of teens admitted to a substance abuse treatment program claim marijuana as their primary drug of abuse.[12] Neither alcohol, tobacco, nor prescription drugs are responsible for over 70 percent of teen substance abuse problems. It is marijuana that has that dubious distinction.

Colorado's Medical Marijuana Experience

What have been the consequences of this explosion in medical marijuana use? Colorado provides a dramatic example of how an initially well-intended medical marijuana program can grow out of control with very negative consequences. This earlier medical program was passed by voters in November 2000. It had limits, and between 2001 and 2008, only 5,993 patient applications for identification cards were submitted. Marijuana "caregivers" who provided the medical marijuana were limited to five patients each. Consequently, there were no dispensaries.

In late 2007, a Denver judge struck down the five-patient limit. In 2009, the US Department of Justice issued its guidelines to US Attorneys in those states that had enacted medical marijuana laws. That memorandum advised the US Attorneys to "not focus federal resources in your state on individuals whose actions are in clear and unambiguous compliance with state laws providing for the medical use of marijuana." The era of medical dispensaries thus began. While much attention has been given to Colorado's full legalization of recreational marijuana, which was fully implemented with the opening of stores on January 1, 2014, the truth is that the advent of medical marijuana dispensaries and the widespread commercialization of marijuana created de facto legalization in 2009. By the end of 2009, patient applications had grown from a total of just under six thousand in the preceding seven years to an additional thirty-eight thousand in just one year. Also, over 250 medical dispensaries emerged, and were allowed to operate as caregivers, without limitations on the number of patients they could claim. There were 532 licensed dispensaries in Colorado and over 108,000 registered patients by 2012. Not surprisingly, 94 percent of these registered patients qualified for their medical marijuana card by claiming "severe pain."

A 2011 study of current marijuana use by twelve- to seventeen-year-olds showed that 10.72 percent of that age group in Colorado used marijuana, compared with the national average usage of 7.04 percent. Also in 2011, the NIDA reported that the average percentage of twelfth graders who had used marijuana in the last thirty days was 22.6 percent. This compared with the Colorado average of 31.2 percent. According to the Colorado Department of Education, the number of drug-related suspensions/expulsions was relatively stable at around 3,800 for each of the academic years ending in 2007, 2008, and 2009. It further reported, however, that those numbers jumped to an average of over 5,100 for the academic years that ended in 2010, 2011, and 2012.

The easy availability of medical marijuana also had consequences for young adults ages eighteen to twenty-five. The National Survey on Drug Use and Health in 2011 showed that for young adults in Colorado, the average past month's marijuana use was 27.26 percent, compared to the national average of 18.78 percent.

A joint study by the National Institute on Alcohol Abuse and

Average Drug-Related Suspensions/Expulsions

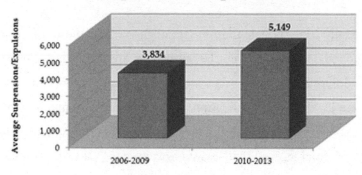

SOURCE: Colorado Department of Education, Academic Years 2006-2013

Alcoholism and NIDA, published in 2014, found "an increased number of marijuana-positive Colorado drivers involved in fatal motor vehicle crashes since Colorado's legalization of medical marijuana in 2009. A similar increase was not seen in the 34 states that did not have medical marijuana laws when this study was conducted."[13] Interestingly, no increase in the number of alcohol-related fatal crashes was found during this time. So much for the argument that "Since alcohol kills more people than marijuana, legalizing marijuana is no big deal." Nationally, marijuana contributed to nearly three thousand traffic fatalities, 12 percent of traffic deaths, in 2010.[14] The National Highway Traffic Safety Administration has found nearly half of fatally injured drivers who tested positive for marijuana were younger than twenty-five.[15] As one of the authors of a Columbia University study put it, "If this trend continues, in five or six years non-alcohol drugs will overtake alcohol to become the most common substance involved in deaths related to impaired driving."[16]

Just why is it there now are so many fatalities related to alcohol as compared to marijuana? Dr. Nora Volkow of NIDA put it well:

> Many more people die of alcohol than all of the illicit drugs together... And it's not because they are more dangerous or addictive. Not at all—they are less dangerous. It's because they are legal... The legalization process generates a much greater exposure of people and hence of negative consequences that will emerge. And that's why I always say, "Can we as a country afford to have a third legal drug? Can we?" We know the costs already on healthcare, we know the costs on accidents, on lost productivity. I let the numbers speak for themselves.[17]

It's not just teens in states with medical marijuana laws who suffer the consequences. Marijuana, like any commodity, does not stay within its own state. Marijuana bought at dispensaries in Colorado and other states has found its way into states where there are no provisions for medical marijuana. Since the commercialization of medical marijuana, there has been a significant increase in marijuana being diverted from Colorado to other states. The El Paso Intelligence Center (EPIC)[18] has established a National Seizure System where seizures of marijuana from Colorado can be reported by police authorities throughout the country. The system is voluntary and by definition, and only includes those shipments that are interdicted, which most interdiction experts estimate represents 10 percent or less of the actual loads of marijuana diverted from Colorado to other states. As can be seen in this chart, the number of seizures has grown dramatically since commercialization in 2009.

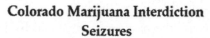

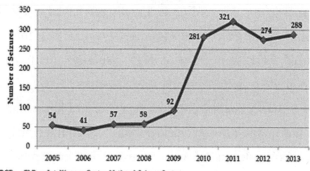

SOURCE: El Paso Intelligence Center, National Seizure System

Such diversions occur not only by car or truck, but also through the US mail and private package services. The US Postal Inspection Service reported an astounding rise in the seizure of packages containing marijuana that originated in Colorado and were destined for other states.

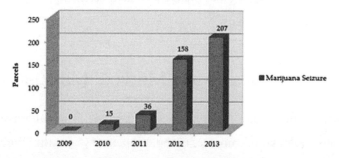

SOURCE: United States Postal Inspection Service – Prohibited Mailing of Narcotics

As with the number of police seizures from vehicles, this chart does not capture packages that were mailed and reached, undetected, their intended out-of-state destinations.

Humans are not the only ones impacted by the wider availability of marijuana. "According to a study published in the *Journal of Veterinary Emergency and Critical Care* in 2012, there has been a fourfold increase in cases of dog poisonings due to marijuana at two Colorado hospitals over the past six years…Two of the reported incidents led to fatalities, including a dog and horse that died after eating marijuana-infused baked goods."[19] Such incidents are not isolated to Colorado. In Arizona, for example, "emergency rooms for pets are seeing more dogs that have eaten marijuana in brownies, cookies, oils and other forms," according to an article in the *Arizona Daily Star.* "People come in and their dogs are lethargic, with their eyes rolling in the back of their heads, or they're unconscious," Dr. Billy Griswold with Emergency Animal Clinic is quoted as saying.[20] Griswold added that over the past few years he has treated at least twenty-four dogs each month that have eaten marijuana. What happens to these dogs? "Unpredictable reactions ranging from depression, staggering and dilated pupils to vomiting, seizures, coma and, in rare cases, death."[21]

The Marketing of Medical Marijuana

Just how medicinal is this drug for humans? One can easily shop for the nearest or most enticing dispensary on the Web. Take

Colorado again, search for "medical marijuana dispensaries" and the Web site WeedMaps gives you dispensaries such as Strawberry Fields Alternative Health, an option in Colorado Springs. This can be replicated in any number of cities. Strawberry Fields promotes "Bubblegum," "Grape Ape," "Skywalker OG," "Voodoo Star," "Northern Lights," "Heavy Duty Fruity," among other flavors. How are these flavors and strains, these so-called medicines, described? Bubblegum: "Very fruity and sweet aroma with a mild hint of bubblegum. Covered in frosted trichomes our bubblegum is a great potent indica. Produces a heavy body high that will have you off your feet and relaxing for hours. Great for patients with multiple sclerosis, bipolar mood swings, muscle relaxer, or for appetite stimulation." Skywalker: "Sour aroma taste of diesel. Heavy hitting and dream like with a pleasant euphoric high. Long lasting and great for sleep and chronic pain." Northern Lights: "Strong body high with mellow head buzz. This one is a creeper. Starts off with a mild racy sativa euphoria and works its way down to the body. Putting you in a moderate couch lock stone." And, one more, Voodoo Star: "This particular strain is one unlike any other. Our most popular and prized strain is Voodoo. The pungent and unique smell of the Voodoo Star will leave you with shock and awe. A delicious taste that stays in your mouth for sometime after being used. Recommended for general relaxation, appetite stimulation, and mild pain/tension relief." Can you imagine a family physician or neighborhood pharmacist recommending "Voodoo Star"?

Of course there are all kinds of strains and flavors that sound more like candy for children than medicine for adults. One can find "Grape God," "Tangerine Haze," "Pineapple Express," and "Blueberry" at Kind Therapeutics, also in Colorado Springs. If these strains, and others, sound like the kinds of things children would go for more than adults, there's a reason for that, just as there is a reason we drive by head shops and dispensaries that have outdoor marketers with signs on the streets at two thirty, three, and three thirty p.m.—not business rush hour, but rush hour for when children leave school. Here are a few pictures of this new medicine:

Bob Berg/Getty

Seth McConnell/Getty

Bob Berg/Getty

Aside from the "Green Crack,"* which is a grotesque appeal to, and conflation of, two dangerous drugs (one more dangerous than the other), one clearly sees the appeal to young people in both the packaging and marketing of this "medicine."

Thus it should be no surprise to find what *JAMA Pediatrics* found: according to an article quoting the *JAMA* study, "When the number of people approved to purchase marijuana for medical use increased sharply in Colorado in 2009, officials witnessed a jump in the number of calls to poison control centers about children inadvertently eating marijuana-laced products, such as brownies, cookies, and candies."[22] The article goes on to say the *JAMA* researchers, comparing "the proportion of marijuana ingestions by young children who were brought to the emergency room before and after

---

*"Crack" is considered by most experts to be the most dangerous and addictive form of cocaine; cities throughout the 1980s and early 1990s suffered from a "crack epidemic" that ravaged their communities and families. It is an odd return to the middle ages of drug abuse in our inner cities to bring back and promote that drug in the public mind.

October 2009, when drug enforcement laws regarding medical marijuana use were relaxed," the *JAMA* researchers found "no record of children brought to the ER in a large Colorado children's hospital for marijuana-related poisonings between January 2005 and September 30, 2009...By comparison, they found 14 cases involving marijuana ingestion between October 1, 2009, and December 31, 2011."[23] Eight of those children, none older than twelve, had consumed "medical marijuana," and all of these had to be admitted to the hospital. While none died, two had to go into intensive care.[24]

Substance use and abuse begins in the teen years. The average age of first-time marijuana use in the country is 17.9 years for all current users of marijuana.[25] The chances that someone will begin using marijuana for the first time after the age of twenty-one are very low. If a dispensary or dealer can get a child hooked, there is a much greater chance of having a client for the long term. This is not a novel strategy: many will recall the societal revulsion caused by tobacco companies marketing to children. Do you remember Joe Camel, a cartoon figure who smoked cigarettes, clearly appealing to youth? He's not around anymore. Society said our children's lungs were too important. We repeat, what of our children's lungs *and* hearts *and* brains?

Dr. Nora Volkow, when asked by a columnist recently, "Isn't tobacco worse than marijuana for teens?," responded:

Wait a second...Nicotine does not interfere with cognitive ability. So if you are an adolescent and you are smoking marijuana and going to school, it's going to interfere with your capacity to learn. So what is worse, as an adolescent right now? To have

basically something that is jeopardizing your development edu-
cationally or to smoke a cigarette that, when you are 60 years of
age, is going to lead to impaired pulmonary function and perhaps cancer?...I would argue that you do not want to mess with
your cognitive capacity, that that is a very large price to pay.[26]

She could have mentioned cardiac function and psychosis as well.
But the point is made: it makes no sense to say that one substance
is worse so we should legalize another unhealthy product. Instead,
protecting our children should be guided by concern for the health
of all their vital functions.

Just how ubiquitous are these dispensaries selling "Green Crack"
and "Voodoo Star" and how much "medicine" is someone allowed
to have? In Denver there are more medical marijuana dispensaries
than there are Starbucks coffee shops.[27] For that matter, there are
more dispensaries than liquor stores or licensed pharmacies.[28] In
Los Angeles, pot stores outnumber the combined total of Starbucks
and McDonald's stores by a ratio of two to one.[29] Medical marijuana
is big business and it is getting bigger.

Every major city has an alternative newspaper, usually a weekly,
commonly distributed for free. Its income is based on advertise-
ments. Increasingly the pages of those ads are for medical marijuana
dispensaries. Let us look at the way "medicine" is now being promoted in America. Take the *Phoenix New Times*. It carries two full
pages of dispensary ads, right in front of the ads for adult escorts.
Here is the text from some of those ads: "New Patients—Get a FREE
Gram with the purchase of 1/8th." "Medical marijuana DELIVERY

Now Available." "Medical Marijuana Evaluations: Walk in Welcome...Get $25.00 Off with this ad." "ARCH Club: New Patients: Receive Free Gram with the purchase of an 1/8th." "Herbal Wellness Clinic: Free Gram & Glass Pipe (First Time Patients Only)."[30]

We are now used to hearing about "Big Tobacco" as a label for companies that sell cigarettes. Why are we not hearing about "Big Marijuana"? Colorado dispensaries reported over $320 million of income in 2013, and in Arizona, the first year medical marijuana was legalized, dispensaries were a $40 million business.[31]

The Absence of Any Meaningful Regulation of Medical Marijuana

As for the dose: how much medical marijuana is one allowed to have? In Colorado one is allowed to possess two ounces of marijuana—that is about 120 joints. In Arizona one may buy up to five ounces a month, approximately 300 joints. In some states, such as California, Michigan, and New Mexico, the limit is higher.[32] Arizona's 300 joints a month is approximately ten joints a day. Neither of the authors, who attended college in the 1960s, ever recall any of our acquaintances smoking anywhere near that quantity. Remember, the average THC level today is more than five times greater than it was in those days. In Colorado and Washington State, however, these "limits" are practically useless. In Colorado it is legal to possess up to an ounce of marijuana for "recreational" use, as it is legal to grow your own plants.[33] In Washington State one can possess up to an ounce—about sixty joints—but can only grow one's own marijuana if one has a "medicinal" need.

Our point is this: as serious as the diseases for which marijuana is used are, is it not confounding (and undermining of the case for medical marijuana) that the dispensing and selling of "medical marijuana" are so unregulated, and its packaging so candy-like? We are told about people who have found no relief from spasms or nausea due to very serious illnesses, and then turn to marijuana. They are thus given an unregulated product with varied strengths based on their own preferences, packaged and marketed like this:

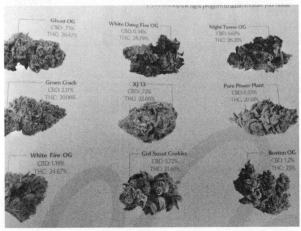

This:

Justin Sullivan/Getty

And these:

Of course, each state has a different set of rules, just as each dispensary offers different strains, flavors, and potencies of THC. It is nearly impossible, with such state-by-state variation and voter-approved "medicine," to take seriously the universal claims of critical need. The "medical marijuana" environment of a wide variety of unregulated products cannot be impressive to medical professionals taking diseases seriously.

The Medical Community and "Medical Marijuana"

Where is the medical community on the use of marijuana as medicine and who are the doctors who are recommending it? Among the expert organizations, the American Psychiatric Association has said this about marijuana as medicine:

> There is no current scientific evidence that marijuana is in any way beneficial for the treatment of any psychiatric disorder. In contrast, current evidence supports, at minimum, a strong association of cannabis use with the onset of psychiatric disorders. Adolescents are particularly vulnerable to harm, given the effects of cannabis on neurological development...
>
> Medical treatment should be evidence-based and determined by professional standards of care; it should not be authorized by ballot initiatives. No medication approved by the FDA is smoked. Marijuana that is dispensed under a state-authorized program is not a specific product with controlled dosages. The buyer has no way of knowing the strength or purity of the product, as cannabis lacks the quality control of FDA-approved medicines.[34]

The American Medical Association voted last year to reaffirm its
official position that "cannabis is a dangerous drug and as such is a
public health concern." The American Society of Addiction Medicine states, "Controlled substances are drugs that have recognized
abuse potential. Marijuana is high on that list because it is widely
abused and a major cause of drug dependence in the United States
and around the world." Interestingly, ASAM continues:

"Cognitive dissonance" is a term that aptly describes the current approach to "medical marijuana." Scientists recognize the
public health harms of tobacco smoking and urge our young
people to refrain from the practice, yet most cannabis consumers use smoking as their preferred delivery mechanism. The
practice of medicine is increasingly evidence-based, yet some
physicians are willing to consider "recommending" cannabis
to their patients, despite the fact that they lack even the most
rudimentary information about the material (composition,
quality, and dose, and no controlled studies provide information on its benefit and safety of its use in chronic medical
conditions). Pharmaceutical companies are responsible for
the harms caused by contaminated or otherwise dangerous
products and tobacco companies can be held accountable for
harms caused by cigarettes, yet, dispensaries distribute cannabis products about which very little is known, including their
source. Efforts are being made to stem the epidemic of prescription drug abuse, including FDA-mandated risk management plans required for prescription medications, yet cannabis

distribution sites proliferate in many states, virtually without regulation.[35]

Cancer? The American Cancer Society's official position is this: "The ACS does not advocate the use of inhaled marijuana or the legalization of marijuana."[36] Glaucoma? The American Ophthalmological Society:

> Marijuana cigarettes also contain hundreds of compounds that damage the lungs, and the deleterious effect of chronic, frequent use of marijuana upon the brain is also well established... Unless a well tolerated formulation of a marijuana-related compound with a much longer duration of action is shown in rigorous clinical testing to reduce damage to the optic nerve and preserve vision, there is no scientific basis for use of these agents in the treatment of glaucoma.[37]

The American Academy of Pediatrics:

> The significant neuropharmacologic, cognitive, behavioral, and somatic consequences of acute and long-term marijuana use are well known and include negative effects on short-term memory, concentration, attention span, motivation, and problem solving, which clearly interfere with learning; adverse effects on coordination, judgment, reaction time, and tracking ability, which contribute substantially to unintentional deaths and injuries among adolescents (especially those associated with motor

vehicles); and negative health effects with repeated use similar to effects seen with smoking tobacco…The American Academy of Pediatrics opposes the legalization of marijuana.[38]

So who are the doctors recommending marijuana? Any doctor can recommend it in a state that has legalized its medicinal use—and in many cases the doctors are wholly out of the field of brain or even lung care: they are obstetricians, general practitioners, and doctors in almost every other specialty, including naturopathic medical doctors (not medical doctors or doctors of osteopathy). Some medical marijuana dispensaries, where the doctors practice and recommend on site, even have games and giveaways—ostensibly to entice, who, adults?[39]

It is worth noting that it is increasingly and tellingly difficult to actually find a psychiatrist to recommend marijuana. As quoted above, the American Psychiatric Association's official statement cites a strong association of cannabis use with the onset of psychiatric disorders and finds that adolescents are particularly vulnerable to harm.[40] As one nationally prominent psychiatrist, Dr. Timothy Jennings, recently put it: "Medical marijuana for the treatment of psychiatric problems is no better than prescribing cigarette smoke to treat lung disease."[41]

When Emotion Trumps Science

Still, we will find doctors who disagree; sometimes they are medical celebrities. One who recently gave credence to the claim of marijuana's medical benefits is Sanjay Gupta, CNN's chief medical correspondent. Here is some of what Dr. Gupta wrote in 2009:

I, like many other doctors, am unimpressed with the proposed legislation, which would legalize marijuana irrespective of any medical condition.

Why do I care? As Dr. Nora Volkow, director of NIDA, puts it, "Numerous deleterious health consequences are associated with [marijuana's] short and long-term use, including the possibility of becoming addicted."

What are other health consequences? Frequent marijuana use can seriously affect your short-term memory. It can impair your cognitive ability (why do you think people call it dope?) and lead to long-lasting depression or anxiety. While many people smoke marijuana to relax, it can have the opposite effect on frequent users. And smoking anything, whether it's tobacco or marijuana, can seriously damage your lung tissue.[42]

In 2013 Dr. Gupta had a change of mind. In fact, he wrote a public "apology" for his erstwhile position. Here is some of his apology:

I apologize because I didn't look hard enough, until now. I didn't look far enough. I didn't review papers from smaller labs in other countries doing some remarkable research, and I was too dismissive of the loud chorus of legitimate patients whose symptoms improved on cannabis.

Still, Dr. Gupta's article is mostly anecdotal. He tells one persua-sive story, for example:

In fact, sometimes marijuana is the only thing that works. Take the case of Charlotte Figi, who I met in Colorado. She started having seizures soon after birth. By age 3, she was having 300 a week, despite being on seven different medications. Medical marijuana has calmed her brain, limiting her seizures to 2 or 3 per month.

I have seen more patients like Charlotte first hand, spent time with them and come to the realization that it is irrespon-sible not to provide the best care we can as a medical commu-nity, care that could involve marijuana.[43]

Every one of us should be able to sympathize with Charlotte Figi's plight. We can think of very few who would deny her whatever it is that helps her, and in cases of true medical need, we agree. Set out later in this chapter, we propose a way to legally provide safe and pure medical marijuana. That said, almost every study we have found on the medicinal effects of marijuana is anecdotal. There are many questions about Dr. Gupta's change of mind that go unan-swered. For example, does Dr. Gupta renounce his agreement with Dr. Nora Volkow above? Why doesn't he address legalization? In his most current piece, he does, however, admit this:

I do want to mention a concern that I think about as a father. Young, developing brains are likely more susceptible to harm from marijuana than adult brains. Some recent studies suggest that regular use in teenage years leads to a permanent decrease in IQ. Other research hints at a possible heightened risk of developing psychosis.

Much in the same way I wouldn't let my own children drink alcohol, I wouldn't permit marijuana until they are adults. If they are adamant about trying marijuana, I will urge them to wait until they're in their mid-20s when their brains are fully developed.[44]

That is hardly a wholesale endorsement of legalizing marijuana. It fails to take into account the movement of marijuana from a dangerous product to what is now marketed as a healthy and helpful product. It further avoids acknowledgment of the widespread use and abuse of marijuana by the young. Finally, while he writes marijuana should only be available for adults, would Dr. Gupta deny it to Charlotte Figi? She is now seven years old.[45] Amazingly, there are now marketed strains of marijuana cleverly named after both Charlotte Figi and Dr. Gupta,[46] "Charlotte's Web" and "Gupta Kush." Going forward, here is the medicine Dr. Gupta can take credit for:

But how do we seriously help the Charlottes of the world? After all, there are a few asterisks on the studies and claims finding "no" medical or therapeutic use, inserted by a handful of experts, perhaps like those cases witnessed by Dr. Gupta. Thus, we propose a modest prescription marijuana protocol.

It is clear that today, the public, in vast numbers, supports some form of "medical marijuana" regimen for those who suffer and claim to need it. Such support runs as high as 85 percent.[47] Usually when pollsters ask about this, they refer to a doctor prescribing marijuana for patients who need it. As we know, that is not how medical marijuana works today: "patients" are not regular patients, but rather walk-ins to a "clinic." The clinic is more of a storefront competing with others for the highest levels of THC with the most attractive or enticing strains and giveaways. "Prescriptions" are not prescriptions at all but "recommendations" and "notes." There is no real limit to the variety of complaints or perceived illnesses these "patients" seek to alleviate with marijuana; nor are there barriers to the marijuana's ending up in the hands of adolescents and others wanting it for recreational use. None of this actually has to be the case.

The Scientific Evidence on Marijuana as Medicine

We recognize what some in the sober and serious medical community have recognized, such as the Institute of Medicine, which, while generally opposing the use of smoked marijuana for medicinal or any other purposes, does recognize that "people have varied

responses to medications, and there will likely always be a subpopulation of patients who do not respond well to other medications."[48]
The Institute of Medicine goes on to say there is a possibility marijuana use "would be moderately well suited for particular conditions, such as chemotherapy-induced nausea and vomiting and
AIDS wasting."[49] Additionally, Drs. Samuel Wilkinson and Deepak
Cyril D'Souza of the Yale School of Medicine wrote in the May
2014 *Journal of the American Medical Association* (*JAMA*) that
"Evidence supporting [marijuana's] efficacy varies substantially
and in general falls short of the standards required for approval of
other drugs by the FDA. Some evidence suggests that marijuana
may have efficacy in chemotherapy-induced vomiting, cachexia
[wasting] in HIV/AIDS patients, spasticity associated with multiple
sclerosis, and neuropathic pain."[50] They also go on to write "the evidence for use in other conditions—including post-traumatic stress
disorder, glaucoma, Crohn's disease, and Alzheimer disease—relies
largely on testimonials instead of adequately powered, double-
blind, placebo-controlled randomized clinical trials."[51]

The idea that medical marijuana can be used for a long laundry
list of conditions, such as we hear about in states that have approved
medical marijuana at the ballot box, is nowhere accepted in serious
scientific literature. Indeed, as Wilkinson and D'Souza write, "The
many conditions for which medical marijuana is approved have
no common etiology, pathophysiology, or phenomenology, raising
skepticism about a common mechanism of action."[52] No one medicine has ever been recommended or used for the number of diseases
and ailments political proponents of medical marijuana say it is a

therapy for. The proponents have turned it into some kind of major miracle drug while, at the same time, the scientific literature finds marijuana either dangerous or of extremely limited use, and often both. However, what of the "subpopulation" of those suffering such things as cachexia, multiple sclerosis spasticity, and vomiting who have found no relief in any other drug or substance? The experts cited above write "some" evidence "suggests" that marijuana "may" have efficacy in three or four circumscribed kinds of cases. There is "a possibility" that marijuana "may" be "moderately well suited" for a few of these conditions. Furthermore, it seems probable that "there will likely always be a subpopulation of patients who do not respond well to other medications."

FDA-Approved Marijuana Drugs

What many people do not know is that since 1985, there has been a prescription form of synthetic marijuana, known as Marinol or dronabinol. Marinol, while man-made, contains many of the same properties as regular, smoked marijuana but is manufactured in a gelatin capsule in various doses. It is not smoked or put into candy bars or brownies. Neither, however, is it used or recommended for, or has it been found to be efficacious for, the full laundry list of conditions those who argue for "medical marijuana" claim smoked marijuana can alleviate. It is primarily prescribed "for treating nausea and vomiting associated with cancer chemotherapy and for treating anorexia associated with weight loss in patients with AIDS."[53] Does Marinol actually work? Again, as with any medicine, there will be a subpopulation that does not respond to its effects. And, because it is swallowed in a capsule, the time it takes to affect nausea or vomiting in a patient is going to vary, and take longer to work than the immediate hit smoked marijuana provides. Inhaled marijuana's effects can begin to work in about fifteen seconds, whereas a dose of Marinol may take upwards of an hour and a half. We would urge those who find no relief for the conditions they suffer from, and want to try smoked or candied marijuana, to first seek Marinol. We further understand that not every medicine is effective in all cases for all patients.

We also are as interested as anyone in this debate as to the conclusions the FDA reaches on Sativex, a spray version of cannabis extract. Sativex, manufactured in Great Britain, has been used in other countries and has been shown to be effective in treating spasticity and some forms of pain. As with Marinol, its method of delivery and manufacture allows for a controlled dose. Although the FDA has fast-tracked its approval process in the United States, as of this writing, it is still being tested. If Sativex is ultimately approved, and joins Marinol as a form of prescription relief, it will be interesting to see if the demands for inhaled or candied marijuana remain unchanged. In other words, the scientific, medical, and government authorizing communities are taking the demands for relief found in marijuana seriously, by putting the active ingredient into standardized pill and aerosol forms. Should Sativex join Marinol, one might think the clamor for smoked and candied marijuana, which has no controlled dosage and no quality control on content or safety and is pretty much self-administered through a loose process of recommendations by naturopathic doctors and chiropractors and a very small minority of the medical community, would subside or be rendered nearly irrelevant.

We shall see. Our best guess is that *if* Sativex is approved, there will actually be little or no reduction in sales of "medical marijuana" by the numerous dispensaries enjoying economic gain. This is because the vast majority of those purchases have nothing to do with medication and are entirely geared toward getting high from the smoked and eaten product rather than obtaining relief from the regimented and truly prescribed medicinal form of it. The purchasers are not so much patients as they are recreational users.

Prescription Marijuana—A Modest Proposal

Still, we recognize that Marinol or Sativex may not be efficacious in all patients—no drug is. (It is an interesting side note that this admission about lack of 100 percent efficacy in legal drugs is almost never made by proponents of smoked or eaten marijuana about their products. Not only is the efficacy of smoked and eaten marijuana vouched for with nearly 100 percent conviction, the list of ailments that smoked and eaten marijuana arguably treats is ever-expanding.) Thus, we propose a medical and political solution. It would require a rigorously monitored process by which these real patients (e.g., those suffering from cachexia and spasticity who have found no relief in other, approved drugs) can obtain what they need. This would be somewhat similar to a program the FDA ran from 1978 until 1992, whereby a small number of patients were given marijuana cigarettes with a known and consistent THC level. Participation in this program had to be approved by the National Institutes of Health, the FDA, and the DEA. Modeled on that Compassionate Investigational New Drug program, we propose the following:

Medical marijuana could be used for certain patients according to the following criteria:

1. A patient can participate in this program only with a special waiver from a physician who attests that other medications have been tried and failed to relieve the condition.
2. The program is limited to those who suffer from those few conditions for which the Institute of Medicine has found some evidence that smoked marijuana may be helpful when other medications have not.
3. Both the patient and physician must sign a formal statement, under penalty of federal perjury charges, attesting to the use of only this marijuana, by only this patient, for only this condition.
4. The patient must also sign a waiver of understanding that the use of marijuana can lead to any number of adverse side effects, releasing the government from any potential liability.
5. The physician, aside from facing perjury charges, is subject to loss of his or her medical license for violation of this protocol.

6. The condition must be chronic, that is to say long-term and not temporary.

7. The government-provided marijuana must be at a standardized dose (the Compassionate Investigational New Drug program used a standardized 3.5 percent THC level).

8. The physician must be a specialist in the field of the disease the patient suffers.

9. A hospital pharmacy must fill the prescription the government approved and the doctor certified.

10. The patient must regularly receive prescriptions based on regular reviews—perhaps weekly or bimonthly—of his or her case by the physician.

A program or set of protocols such as the foregoing could do much to solve the true problems suffering patients now have, while at the same time remove the potential for abuse and diversion to adolescent and other recreational populations. Doctors and scientists would be able to see how efficacious marijuana actually is. There could no longer be any claim that opposition to marijuana is political, as this plan challenges the vast number of people clamoring for legalization for therapeutic purposes. It puts a substance that may be helpful, but has great potential for abuse, exclusively into the hands of doctors and true patients. This proposal, we believe, should and could be embraced by both sides of this debate. We might call this "prescription marijuana." That would distinguish it from the "medical marijuana" label that has been put on what many see as a bad joke, giving this product and process the seriousness true patients say they need and deserve.*

Such a regimen also would cause the US Attorney General to demand and ensure closure of all medical marijuana facilities based on the enforcement of federal law. Indeed, this program would likely not work if medical marijuana dispensaries continued to operate. At the end of the day, we have taken seriously the medical issues and patient frustration and provided a safe and accessible protocol for the dispensing of a potentially beneficial substance to that small part of the population certain scientific and medical communities suggest may be helped. This is both a political and a medical solution to the debate over "medical marijuana." In sum, those who truly might benefit from it can get it, almost like any other true medication dispensed by prescription, and those who oppose such a program need to be asked, "Why?"

It is important to recognize the rigor of such a program, just as it was important to have the scientific community test Marinol before it went to market, just as it is important to await the results of the approval process that has now been "fast-tracked" for Sativex. Those researchers and physicians who have published their concerns about smoked or eaten marijuana in such

---

*We do not suggest reclassifying marijuana from a Schedule I drug to a Schedule II drug. Rather, in this "prescription marijuana" program, we suggest the DEA issue a waiver to the physicians who prescribe it under the program, perhaps with a separate prescription pad issued to them with a separate DEA number from the one they use for their regular prescriptions.

journals as the *Journal of the American Medical Association*, the *New England Journal of Medicine*, and elsewhere all caution that medicine—true, therapeutic, safe, and efficacious medicine—is not and cannot be subject to a vote. Medicine, like disease, is serious business. Its recognition, use, deployment, and method of delivery should not be determined by popular demand. We do that with no other medical treatment, not even over-the-counter non-prescription drugs. As doctors Wilkinson and D'Souza put it in the *JAMA*:

> If marijuana is to be used for medical purposes, it should be subjected to the same evidence-based review and regulatory oversight as other medications prescribed by physicians. Potentially therapeutic compounds of marijuana should be purified and tested in randomized, double-blind, placebo- and active-controlled clinical trials. Toward this end, the federal government should actively support research examining marijuana's potentially therapeutic compounds. These compounds should be approved by the FDA (not by popular vote or state legislature), produced according to good manufacturing practice standards, distributed by regulated pharmacies, and dispensed via a conventional and safe route of administration (such as oral pills or inhaled vaporization). Otherwise, states are essentially legalizing recreational marijuana but forcing physicians to act as gatekeepers for those who wish to obtain it.[54]

Our modest proposal does go one step further, of course. We are willing to try, and have outlined a method to effectuate, a physician-based regimen for inhaled marijuana. It will be interesting to see whether, if this proposal is adopted, the call for dispensaries and unregulated use ceases. We know the dangers of "medicine by vote" from our recent history. Laetrile was that example. Promoted as a cure for cancer, Laetrile was made from apricot and peach pits. It was never approved by the FDA, and many sought it in Mexico and elsewhere. Indeed, some twenty US states voted to approve its use throughout the 1970s,[55] but to no therapeutic avail, and several people died of cyanide poisoning as a result of using Laetrile. Most importantly, though, cancer patients suffered, not only from false hopes and promises, but from the distraction of using a quack medicine as an alternative to scientifically researched and recommended standard medicines used to treat cancer. As one British doctor put it, "Testimonials are not science."[56]

We believe our proposal can resolve much of the debate, while getting the desired marijuana into the hands of those who may truly need it, just as Dr. Gupta suggests. Still, in the main, we are cautious because the idea that medical marijuana was always about therapeutic medicine, or ever was, is belied by the former executive director of the largest marijuana legalization advocacy organization in America, the National Organization for the Reform of Marijuana Laws (NORML), Richard Cowan. Mr. Cowan is on record and video as saying, "The key is medical access, because once you have hundreds of thousands of people using marijuana under medical supervision, the whole scam is going to be brought up...Then we will get medical, then we will get full legalization."[57] Colorado got the message.

Chapter 3

Legalization and Its Effects

Those who have experimented with legalization and decriminalization of marijuana laws have come to regret it. The state of Alaska is a telling and complicated case in point. In 1982 the state decriminalized the possession of marijuana for those over nineteen years of age. Yet by 1990 the residents of the state had had enough of that experiment. Among other problems, "the state's 12 to 17-year-olds used marijuana at more than twice the national average for their age group."[1] Here again, the law was meant for adults, but use among children went up. In 1990, Alaskans voted to recriminalize marijuana possession, by a vote of 54.3 percent to 43.7 percent.[2] Alaskans defeated a re-legalization measure in 2000 by a vote of nearly 60 percent to 40 percent.[3] In 2004, another attempt to legalize marijuana in Alaska failed. However, memories are short, and now that the pro-legalization movement has marshaled its resources and grown, in

2014, Alaska once again put a full legalization measure on the ballot. The campaign to legalize in Alaska received a $200,000 infusion of support from the Marijuana Policy Project.[4] Indeed, the legalization measure was passed in November 2014.

One need not look back to the Alaskan experience to refresh memories. Already we can see what is taking place in Colorado. The negative effects are not just hitting children. Like Laurie Roberts of the *Arizona Republic*, Maureen Dowd experienced a dose of buyer's remorse, and a lot of other bad things, too. A liberal columnist for the *New York Times*, Ms. Dowd "nibbled off the end and then, when nothing happened, nibbled some more" of a marijuana-laced candy bar she'd bought at a Denver-area pot shop.[5] "What could go wrong with a bite or two?" she thought. "Everything, as it turned out."[6]

I felt a scary shudder go through my body and brain. I barely made it from the desk to the bed, where I lay curled up in a hallucinatory state for the next eight hours. I was thirsty but couldn't move to get water. Or even turn off the lights. I was panting and paranoid…I strained to remember where I was or even what I was wearing, touching my green corduroy jeans and staring at the exposed-brick wall. As my paranoia deepened, I became convinced that I had died and no one was telling me.

It took all night before it began to wear off, distressingly slowly. The next day, a medical consultant at an edibles plant where I was conducting an interview mentioned that candy bars like that are supposed to be cut into 16 pieces for novices; but that recommendation hadn't been on the label.[7]

"Hadn't been on the label." Exactly. One wonders, if a warning were on the label, whether that would entice others to go for the additional "high" or convince them to keep their "dose" low. Such a label may have saved Ms. Dowd from being convinced she had died; others could just as easily seek greater and greater highs. Indeed, given the way we know the brain adjusts to doses, seeking and needing ever more, that would likely be the case for most regular users. If the word *dangerous* does not seem appropriate here, we cannot think of a case where it would.

Adults like Ms. Dowd, though, are not our main concern. She is beyond the age of initiation, and addiction is unlikely to become an ongoing problem for her. Our concern is the younger, innocent population. As the science writer David DiSalvo puts it, "Going even a little overboard [with marijuana, as Ms. Dowd did] can send a novice brain into a whirlwind."[8] That is the brain we care most about, the novice brain.

Some Unintended Consequences of Legalization

The journal *Slate*, while reporting on some of the economic benefits to the Colorado government from sales of marijuana, titled its article "Going to Pot?" because it detailed what it called many of the "unintended consequences" of the state's new legalization regime. Unintended, possibly; unexpected, not really. "So-called edibles are being blamed for an increase in the number of pot-related emergency room visits, including those from a half-dozen or so children who unknowingly ate pot-laced treats."[9]

Since the de facto and actual legalization of marijuana in Colorado, some users who are not satisfied by the THC content of the average marijuana cigarette have sought a more euphoric high. Hence, they have developed laboratories known as butane hash oil (BHO) labs to extract the THC. The process entails forcing butane through an extraction tube, which is filled with marijuana that has been finely ground. The result is a product consisting of butane and a very high concentration of THC. Once the butane has completely evaporated, there is a viscous mass. The product frequently has a THC concentration ranging from 60 to 90 percent. This hash oil is consumed by smoking, or more commonly by vaporization called *dabbing*. The manufacturing process is extremely dangerous, as butane is a very volatile and explosive solvent. For example:

Colorado authorities are also dealing with a rash of fiery house explosions caused by pot enthusiasts making THC-rich hash oil in their homes through a dangerous process that involves heavy amounts of butane, a highly flammable gas that can linger and ignite. Earlier this week in a suburb of Colorado Springs, firefighters responded to one such explosion at an apartment and found two adults and a 3-year-old child trapped inside.[10]

In addition, "Hash oil–making is believed to have caused a blast that destroyed a townhouse. All told, firefighters have responded to more than 30 such explosions this year [the first half of 2014] already, roughly three times the number from all of last year, according to the Rocky Mountain High Intensity Drug Trafficking Area agency."[11] The HIDTA is a drug-prohibition enforcement program run by the Office of National Drug Control Policy, whose mission is to enhance and coordinate America's drug control efforts among local, state, and federal law enforcement agencies. Not unexpectedly, as the number of BHO lab explosions have increased, so have the resulting injuries.

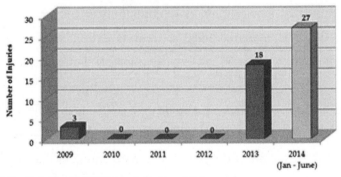

Colorado Reported THC Extraction Lab Explosion Injuries

SOURCE: Rocky Mountain HIDTA Investigative Support Center

Then there are the two Denver deaths, one of a nineteen-year-old who jumped to his death while high, the other of a woman whose husband shot her after eating "Karma Kandy."[12] Even more from a recent *New York Times* report: "Sheriffs in neighboring states complain about stoned drivers streaming out of Colorado and through their towns" and "nine children have ended up at Children's Hospital

Colorado in Aurora after consuming marijuana, six of whom got critically sick."[13] This is not so surprising when you find a fourth grader in Greely selling his grandmother's pot brownies to fellow students on the playground, as was reported this past April.[14]

There also has been a sizable increase in marijuana-related DUI admissions to treatment centers.

Arapahoe House is Colorado's largest provider of community detox services with three centers located across metro Denver in Aurora, Commerce City and Wheat Ridge. New data showing the number of clients driving under the influence (DUI) of marijuana from January 1–May 31, 2014 compared to the same time period in 2013 indicates admissions have nearly doubled from 8 percent to 15 percent since recreational legalization went into effect.[15]

The truth is that Colorado is about to wreak a great deal of havoc, and we do not think the mainstream media gets it. A recent CNN report on the recreational use of marijuana in Colorado found the following: just since last year, "thousands of strains of marijuana have hit the market"; "business is booming." One shop reported ten thousand customers a month, a large percentage of whom came from out of state. But when the CNN reporter showed one of the more popular strains on television, with the clumps of marijuana in her hand, someone at the network transposed lights and sparkles onto her hand as well, to show the "magic" and euphoric effect that strain's producers advertise. It looked like Tinker Bell in a Disney production, enticing and desirable. The story glamorized the product.[16] Not everyone shares this rose-colored glasses perspective. In October 2014, Colorado Governor John Hickenlooper, a Democrat, was asked during a debate what he would say to other states considering similar measures. His response: "I'm not saying it was reckless because I'll get quoted everywhere, but if it was up to me I wouldn't have done it, right? I opposed it from the very beginning. In matter of fact, all right what the hell, I'll say it was reckless."[17]

Dear Bill:

I wanted to relate to you my family's experience with drug abuse and its consequences. My wife and I live in Colorado and are firmly against the state's legalization of marijuana. It was dismaying, to say the least, when the law was passed not by a small margin in 2012.

Our son, the middle child of three, started using marijuana in middle school in the mid 1990s. We firmly believe in the "gateway" aspect of the drug as he progressed to experimentation with ecstasy, cocaine, and considerable consumption of alcohol in high school. It got so bad that in his junior year we were forced to intervene. We sent him, against his wishes, to a seven-week rehab in the woods and then directly on to a therapeutic shelter.

In the past we've gotten/forced him into multiple rehabilitation programs, none of which he successfully completed. He's now 30, has a girlfriend, and has a decent job here in Colorado. My wife and I would agree that he's

Marijuana marketed to look like familiar candy bars—
does anyone really believe such packaging
isn't targeting kids?

Bloomberg/Getty

Kathryn Scott Osler/Getty

The New Medicine

Justin Sullivan/Getty

Bob Berg/Getty

Bob Berg/Getty

This is how medical marijuana is being advertised in Colorado

Seth McConnell/Getty

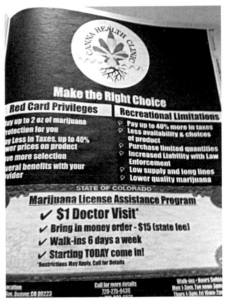

Targeting out-of-state skiers, and more sodas and candy

Past Month Use by 12 to 17-Year-Olds Medical Marijuana States vs. Non-Medical Marijuana States

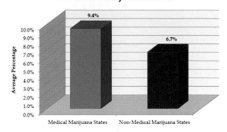

SOURCE: Data from SAMHSA.gov, National Survey on Drug Use and Health, 2013

Average Drug-Related Suspensions/Expulsions

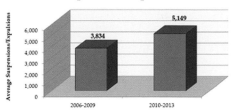

SOURCE: Colorado Department of Education, Academic Years 2006-2013

Parcels Containing Marijuana Mailed from Colorado to Another State

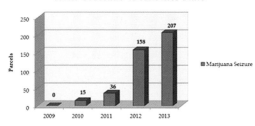

SOURCE: United States Postal Inspection Service – Prohibited Mailing of Narcotics

Colorado Marijuana Interdiction Seizures

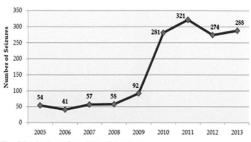

SOURCE: El Paso Intelligence Center, National Seizure System

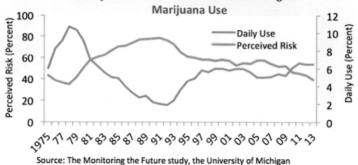

Percentage of U.S. 12 Grade Students Reporting Daily Marijuana Use vs. Perceived Risk of Regular Marijuana Use

Source: The Monitoring the Future study, the University of Michigan

Illegal Drug Use in America 1979 – 2009

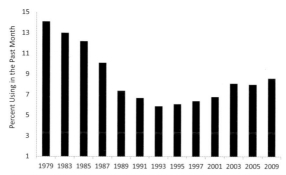

Source: Authors' reproduction based on Substance Abuse and Mental Health Services Administration Center for Behavioral Health Statistics and Quality, *National Survey on Drug Use and Health* (formerly the *National Household Survey on Drug Abuse*)

Colorado Reported THC Extraction Lab Explosion Injuries

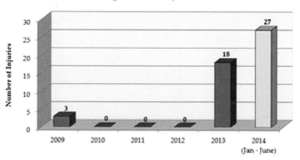

SOURCE: Rocky Mountain HIDTA Investigative Support Center

Marijuana dispensary displays selling marijuana by name—from Girl Scout Cookies to Gupta Kush

Hyping marijuana based on increased potency—
the selling of Turbo Pot

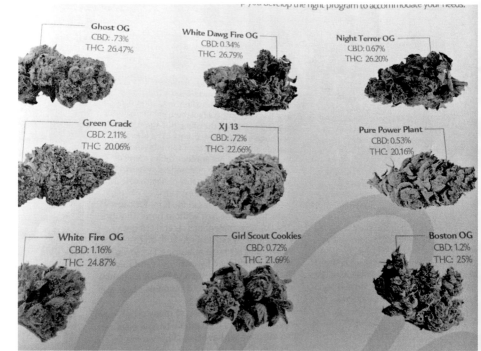

currently a functional substance abuser with a dark side that we find hard to penetrate.

The effects have been costly. Besides the tens of thousands of dollars we spent in various programs, the impact on relationships within the family have been consequential. His siblings want the best for him but they are many times wary of his motives. Our marital relationship has suffered and at one point we separated briefly, fifteen years ago because of disagreements in how to handle our situation.

Let no one say that marijuana is just a simple, no-risk additive to the pleasure levers of life. The legalization step is a serious and a dangerous development for our culture. My personal conviction is that Colorado will rue the day that this law was passed.

Karl in CO

Legalization's Effect on Youth Drug Use

We know that the three factors that most affect youth drug use are perceived risk/social acceptability, availability, and cost. Legalization will negatively affect all three factors.

Legality changes the cultural perception of the risks and acceptability of marijuana usage, particularly among the young. As Drs. Robert DuPont and Herbert Kleber have pointed out, "The Monitoring the Future survey, conducted by the University of Michigan since 1975, found that the rate of marijuana use in youths is inversely related to 'perceived risk' and 'perceived social disapproval.' "[18] As perceived risk goes up, use goes down; as perceived social disapproval goes up, use goes down. Turning marijuana into medicine, making heroes and punch lines out of dealers of marijuana on television and in movies, legalizing its recreational use, refusing to enforce the laws on it, having news reports depict marijuana with sparkles and lights as if it were magic, all contribute toward lowering not only perceived risk, but also social disapproval. When the President of the United States makes jokes about drug abuse (speaking about the White House pastry chef's excellent pies recently, the President told a group, "I don't know what he does—whether he puts crack in them")[19] or compares marijuana to alcohol and cigarettes, the perception of danger drops even lower and use goes up even higher:

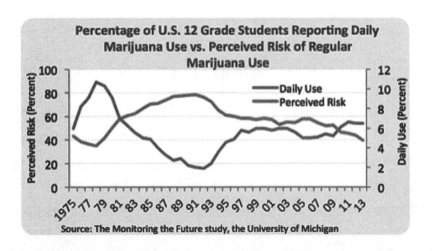

Source: The Monitoring the Future study, the University of Michigan

As the White House's Office of National Drug Control Policy states on its own Web site, "Legality increases the availability and acceptability of drugs."[20]

Legalization will most certainly increase availability. The number of marijuana dispensaries exploded when some limitations on medical marijuana were removed. Full legalization will only lead to an ever-growing number of marijuana stores. Also, as supply grows, the cost will go down, leading to more usage by our youth.

Big Marijuana—The Need to Create Abuse and Dependence

There is an even darker truth to legalization. We know that among consumers of alcohol, the top 10 percent (the heaviest drinkers) imbibe 50 percent of total alcohol consumed, and that the top 20 percent accounts for 80 percent of alcohol consumption. Profits in the legal alcohol business are driven by heavy use of alcohol. Tobacco profits also are driven by heavy users. The widespread usage of tobacco is a phenomenon of the late nineteenth and twentieth centuries. Before the arrival of Big Tobacco companies, cigarettes were hand-rolled. The large tobacco companies created uniform, pre-rolled and packaged cigarettes produced on a mass scale. Having delivered greater supply, these companies set out to increase demand through mass marketing. It worked well for Big Tobacco's bottom line, but not so well for the health of Americans.

Profits in the legal marijuana business likewise will be driven by heavy users. As was written by Professors Mark A. R. Kleiman, Jonathan P. Caulkins, and Angela Hawken in their book *Drugs and Drug Policy*:

> When we create a licit industry selling an abusable drug, the resulting businesses will have a strong profit incentive to create and sustain abusive consumption patterns, because people with substance-abuse disorders consume most of the product. Supplying moderate or controlled use is merely a side business. So if we create a licit cannabis or cocaine industry, we should expect the industry's product design, pricing and marketing to be devoted to creating as much addiction as possible. If you think that marketing executives earn their large salaries, and TV networks earn their huge per-second rates for advertising time, by actually influencing consumption decisions, that thought should give you chills.[21]

Importantly, those most susceptible to addiction are the young.

We know the costs to individuals and society of excessive alcohol and tobacco use. According to the authors of the preceding quote, because of increased availability, much lower prices, and decreases in stigma and personal risks (such as the risk of arrest), legalization of marijuana could mean "four to six times as much cannabis to be consumed after legalization as is consumed now."[22] That number could of course be lower, but given what we know of the direction legalization, de-stigmatization, and reduced perceived harm have already had on consumption, it could be much higher as well. Already saddled with Big Alcohol and Big Tobacco, can we really afford the personal, health, and economic costs that will necessarily follow from legalized Big Marijuana? We all should be very afraid.

Chapter 4

Drug War Myths

A
s with any public policy debate, there are going to be disagreements over ultimate conclusions. The social scientist Irving Kristol is credited with saying: "The first rule of politics is that others may not always agree with you." We would do well to remember that in this and other public policy debates. What we are trying to point out in this book is that while there may be reasons for legalizing marijuana, we believe most—not all, but most—advocates have come to their conclusions in favor of legalization because of an absence of information and through a series of misunderstandings.

Some of those misunderstandings have been the result of deliberate falsehoods promulgated by interest groups. Some have resulted from arguments that contravene conventional wisdom and common sense, but are seized upon by those who would rather get high than critically think about the negative results of their positions or desires. Some simply do not know history very well, or are misinformed about the potency of today's marijuana. Not all of this misunderstanding is deliberate; some arises from a lack of honest information.

We take most of the arguments on behalf of legalization without prejudice and/or attribution of motive, and simply attempt to answer, respond to, or correct them so that a full understanding and debate can be had. We believe that without this debate, without these responses to the tide of the culture right now, America will change drastically for the worse. It will begin with the most vulnerable among us, the youth. We wholeheartedly stand in opposition to harming our youth with a series of experiments that testing, medicine, science, and common sense have already proven dangerous failures.

The Political Debate

The debate, as we stated earlier, does not fall on a standard left-right continuum: some of the most ardent opponents of legalization are Democrats, and some of the most ardent supporters are Republicans. Some of the conservative support for legalization relies on libertarian philosophies, some on states' rights beliefs. The more liberal-oriented support for legalization stems from certain beliefs in personal autonomy, and some is based on beliefs about the justice system. Almost none of the supporters of legalization of marijuana claim that smoking marijuana is without risk, but many supporters minimize or ignore the risks. Some go so far as to claim marijuana's therapeutic properties outweigh its harms. Where the liberal and conservative supporters of legalization tend to agree is on the point of the futility of prohibition. They tend to think the "war on drugs" cannot be won and that prohibition was a failure with alcohol and is being proven so again with drugs. Further, they will argue that what we do legalize already (alcohol, for example) is far more dangerous than marijuana. Thus, the argument goes, it is hypocritical to make illegal a substance safer than what is already legal. Finally, they argue that a legal regimen of taxation and oversight will drive cartels out of business and be a strong source of revenue for the state.

As for the conservative viewpoint, in January 2014 the *National Review*, the flagship journal of the conservative movement, founded by William F. Buckley Jr., published an unsigned editorial from "the editors," speaking on behalf of the journal itself. The title was "Sensible on Weed." The editorial called Colorado's decision to legalize marijuana for recreational purposes "prudent."[1]

The editors then rehashed many of the usual arguments on behalf of legalization, as summarized above. For example, they wrote:

> Marijuana is a drug, as abusable as any intoxicant is, and its long-term use is in some people associated with undesirable effects. But its effects are relatively mild, and while nearly half of American adults have smoked marijuana, few develop habits, much less habits that are lifelong (in another context, we might write "chronic"). Compared to binge drinking or alcohol addiction, marijuana use is a minor public-health concern. All that being the case, the price of prohibition is relatively

high, whether measured in police and penal expenses or in liberty lost. The popularity of marijuana may not be the most admirable social trend of our time, but it simply is not worth suppressing.[2]

However, in the very next paragraph, the editors wrote:

One of the worst consequences of marijuana use is the development of saucer-eyed arguments about the benefits of legalizing it. Colorado, and other states that may follow its example, should go into this with realistic expectations. If the Dutch example is any guide, then Colorado can probably expect to see higher rates of marijuana use and the use of other drugs, though not dramatically so. As with the case of Amsterdam, Colorado already is developing a marijuana-tourism industry—some hotels are considering offering designated marijuana-smoking rooms, even while smoking tobacco outdoors is banned in parts of Boulder—which brings problems of its own, among them opportunistic property crime and public intoxication. Colorado's legal drug dealers inevitably will end up supplying black markets in neighboring prohibition states. Expected tax revenues from marijuana sales will amount to a mere three-tenths of 1 percent of the state's budget.[3]

So even the conservative case for legalization carries with it the admission that legalization will bring with it greater use, more property crime, and more public intoxication, and that the tax revenues gained will be minimal. The moment conservatives start actually supporting policies they admit will lead to more crime is the moment we must ask, "How is this conservative?" Although the conservative movement has many variations, the idea of being "tough on crime," and protecting the safety of citizens and property, has always been a conservative staple. It certainly was one of the main reasons William Buckley ran for mayor of New York City in 1965. Even most liberals would not like to admit to supporting a policy that a priori would lead to more crime.

Conservatives generally favor a state's right to experiment with social and economic policies that impact that state's residents. Massachusetts enacted a sweeping health care policy in 2006 ("Romneycare"), but that program applied only to the residents of Massachusetts. The same cannot be said of a state's legalization of marijuana.

It cannot be considered a state's right to decide for itself what its mores and policies should be on marijuana, when even the legal drug dealers will fuel "black markets in neighboring prohibition states." So much for the "prohibition states'" rights and for marijuana legalization in a few states being an experiment. The states do not have walls. There could be no greater modern example of nullification, actually, than one state's deciding not to legalize marijuana, but then having to take on the effects of legalization from another state. A midyear review of legal marijuana sales in Colorado revealed that 44 percent of all sales in the metro areas of Colorado were to non-Colorado residents, while 90 percent of sales in ski resort areas were to non-residents.[4] One simply cannot contain one state's marijuana within its borders, as the *National Review* editors admit, and as we have already seen.

Bill,

I'm a Trooper with the Highway Patrol (26 years) stationed along I-70. We have had several issues with people going to Colorado to smoke marijuana and coming back through Kansas. Four young men from central KS went to Colorado to "legally" smoke marijuana (never mind that they were under 21). Left to return home after smoking and the driver left the roadway, went through the right-of-way fence, sideswiped one tree and "center punched" a second. When the car struck the tree it spun it around counterclockwise and then flipped onto its top. The three passengers had minor injuries, the driver was hospitalized. Luckily they were all wearing seat belts. Marijuana and paraphernalia were located in the vehicle, all four stated the reason for the trip to Colorado was to smoke pot.

Another Trooper worked one where a father took his grown daughter and some of her friends to Colorado to share the experience. Dad "fell asleep," went into the median where the vehicle rolled, sending all the occupants to the hospital. WHAT A DAD!

The consequences of Colorado's legalization of marijuana can not be measured in Colorado accidents/issues alone. This affects us all.

On a lighter note...

Stopped a vehicle westbound towards Colorado for an equipment violation. Kansas registration from the Kansas City area. Single male driver, 22 years old. Asked where he was headed. "Colorado." Where in Colorado? "Denver." What's going on in Denver? "A funeral." I wrote the ticket and went back to the driver and repeated the questions with the same answers. Then I asked, Whose funeral? "A friend." What do you plan to wear to the funeral? (He was wearing blue jeans and T-shirt and there was no luggage in the vehicle.) "Suit." Where is your suit? "It's already there." After some discussion as to the believability of this I said: So, where are you headed? "Manhattan." (Geography lesson—Manhattan is between KC and Hays—BACK THE OTHER DIRECTION.) When I gave a quizzical response to this he stated, "Seems like the best thing to do right now." After a lengthy discussion it turns out he is a student at Kansas State and had pooled some money together from some friends and was taking a road trip to Colorado to buy marijuana to bring back to campus. His major is entrepreneurship.

The story is a lot longer and more detailed than that, but you get the point.

Bill in KS

Public intoxication is another problem. We do not live in Mayberry, where the town drunk is no more harmful than a neighbor's barking dog. Quite the opposite is true. Public intoxication, whether with alcohol or marijuana, is actually quite dangerous and sometimes deadly. More than 10 percent of fatal car crashes involve marijuana use, a tripling over the past decade, according to a recent study from the Columbia University Mailman School of Public Health.[5] The lead author of the study pointed out, "If a driver is under the influence of alcohol, their risk of a fatal crash is 13 times higher than the risk of the driver who is not under the influence of alcohol...But if the driver is under the influence of both alcohol and marijuana, their risk increased to 24 times that of a sober person." This statistic should be especially interesting to those who say that since alcohol is more deadly or dangerous than marijuana, marijuana should be legalized. Making alcohol use more deadly by the addition of marijuana—with twenty-four times the risk faced by a sober person, compared to thirteen times the risk without marijuana—is not a desideratum any sane person should maintain.

Outside of auto accidents, the argument that marijuana is not dangerous or deadly is simply fallacious. As was reported by the Associated Press on April 18, 2014:

> This week, two Denver deaths were linked to marijuana use, and while some details of the deaths have yet to emerge, they are the first ones on record to be associated with a once-illegal drug that Colorado voters legalized for recreational use, as of January 1, 2014.
>
> One man jumped to his death after consuming a large amount of marijuana contained in a cookie, and in the other

case, a man allegedly shot and killed his wife after eating marijuana candy.[6]

The idea that marijuana only relaxes someone, and does not hype up or excite him or her (nobody can claim it doesn't impair someone), *may once* have been true in small doses and at low levels of THC. We emphasize "may." But it simply is not true today. One cannot predict a body's (or brain's) reaction to marijuana, especially for a first-time user: "The thing to realize is the THC that is present in edibles is a drug like any drug, and there's a spectrum of ways in which people respond," said Michael Kosnett, a medical toxicologist on the clinical faculty at the University of Colorado School of Medicine.

He further observed that a person's genetic makeup, health issues, and other factors can make a difference, and that first-time users might consume too much, unaware of how their bodies will react.[7]

Dear Bill:

Re: legalizing pot. I am a licensed social worker in both SC and NY, working at a state technical college in SC. People who argue that pot is safe, not a gateway drug, etc., are simply misrepresenting the truth. I have worked with many students who are depressed, anxious, etc., and have used pot to self-medicate. Many realize that this is not helping them to cope and that it is actually exacerbating their problems, not to mention that it is illegal, which poses even more issues. Additionally, all of them that have progressed on to the "hard" drugs have used pot first. They simply do not understand that they do not need drugs and alcohol to have a pleasant social experience. The country is sending a dangerous message to our youth, the future leaders of America.

All the best,

Elisa in SC

Marijuana's Potentially Deadly Effects

It simply confounds us as to why people claim marijuana is not deadly. Agreed: marijuana has not been documented to be as directly fatal through overdose as alcohol has. However, it also has been consumed much less due to its general unavailability up until recently. Marijuana has been found:

**to cause deadly strokes in adolescent males ("They developed primary cerebellar infarctions within days after [marijuana use] that could not be attributed to supratentorial herniation syndromes and only minimally involved brainstem structures," according to an article in the *Journal of Pediatrics*);[8]

**to cause acute cardiovascular deaths in young adults ("Very recent cannabis ingestion was documented by the presence of tetrahydrocannabinol (THC) in postmortem blood samples. A broad toxicological blood analysis could not reveal other drugs. Similar cases have been reported in the literature, but the toxicological analysis has been absent or limited to urine samples, which represent a much broader time window for cannabis intake. This paper presents six case reports, where cannabis alone was detected in blood," according to an article in the *Forensic Science International*);[9]

**to be responsible for over 450,000 emergency department (or ED) visits per year;[10]

**to cause fatal automobile accidents ("After alcohol, THC (delta-9-tetrahydrocannabinol), the active ingredient in marijuana, is the substance most commonly found in the blood of impaired drivers, fatally injured drivers, and motor vehicle crash victims," according to the National Institute on Drug Abuse—which also says that motor vehicle accidents are the leading cause of death among people aged 16 to 19);[11]

**to cause "a twofold increase in the risk of an [automobile] accident if there is any measurable amount of THC in the bloodstream," according to a doctor quoted in a *New York Times* article;[12]

**to be the substance most used by teens admitted into substance abuse treatment programs, according to those teens;[13] and

**as documented in the first chapter, to cause numerous and permanent changes to the adolescent brain, affecting everything from IQ to the onset of psychosis, depression, and other neurological pathologies.

The point is this: there is no level of marijuana use that is actually completely safe. As was reported in the *Journal of Neuroscience* in a study published in 2014, even the casual use of marijuana changes the brain.[14] It is puzzling that the editors of the *National Review* are able to say legalization is "prudent," while admitting use will go up. Thus our culture now labels "prudent" and even mostly benign the expanded numbers of injuries, deaths, and brain-adverse pathology that will be caused by legalization, never mind the crime the editors of *National Review* also admit it will fuel.

Law Enforcement and Marijuana

What of the argument that the prohibition of marijuana costs billions in enforcement, and causes hundreds of thousands of arrests each year? Let's examine the numbers from the American Civil Liberties Union (ACLU), which ardently supports the legalization of marijuana. In its 2013 landmark study, it found that the enforcement costs of the prohibition of marijuana by all fifty states combined were between $1.2 billion and $3.6 billion annually.[15] That's about one-seventh to one half of what the United States pays to the United Nations.[16] Understood another way, it is approximately the amount of additional net worth Warren Buffett obtained in one day in March, and about twenty times less than his total net worth.[17] It is a lot of money, but is it an outrageous sum to fight an illegal drug that causes a lot of damage? It is about half the entire budget of Rhode Island, taking the ACLU at its highest estimate—and that $3.6 billion is not per state, it's all states combined.[18] All states combined spent six times less than Colorado's entire budget to fight the most commonly used illegal drug in America. Is that really outrageous?

What is the price of enforcement of the marijuana laws, if one includes the federal portion? At all levels of government, from city to federal, one proponent of legalization pegged the cost at approximately $11 billion.[19] Others, such as Harvard economist Jeffrey Miron (a proponent of legalization), have put it somewhat lower, in the $8 billion range. While $8 billion is a lot of money, it is a third of the entire state budget of Pennsylvania, a thirteenth of the entire California state budget, a quarter of the net worth of one of Google's co-founders, and a sixth of the cost of the most recent Olympics. This is a substantial sum, but it cannot be said that it is prohibitive. Consider the price we would pay if we did not enforce marijuana laws. What would more marijuana use in America look like? What would it cost for more teens in substance abuse treatment, more dropouts from high school, more crime, more ER visits, more traffic accidents and fatalities, and more neurological pathology in our youth? And what would be the price in lost productivity?

Dear Bill,

I spent 30-plus years working with high school students and much of my work was with adolescents who had motivational or behavioral issues. The influence of drugs, particularly marijuana, on young people is inarguable. That influence is nothing but bad. Drug use steals the sense of joy and enthusiasm from kids about their schoolwork and their futures. Time after time, it was my experience that when kids could be moved away from smoking marijuana, they did better in school and at home... People who argue for legalization, or who deny the impact of substance abuse, have never watched someone they care about throw away their future because of drug use. I have numerous specific stories I could relay to you if you wished.

Dave in FL

We cannot point to real numbers for the costs of the fallout from further legalization, but we can presume they all would go up. As Kevin Sabet, a former advisor to President Barack Obama, has written, "Accidents would increase, healthcare costs would rise and productivity would suffer. Legal alcohol serves as a good example: The $8 billion in tax revenue generated from that widely used drug does little to offset the nearly $200 billion in social costs attributed to its use."[20] What of the destruction to families? Most readers of this book know of a family that lost a family member to addiction. The parade of horror is almost too long to detail, from staying up all hours worrying to multiple visits to hospitals and rehab clinics, to stolen property, to the toll on marriages and siblings, and to the heartache of witnessing the wasted potential of a loved one. It is nearly impossible to attribute numbers to these very real costs, but ask a family member of a marijuana addict whether society should continue to fund efforts to reduce marijuana use and abuse, and most will quickly say yes.

As for the hundreds of thousands we arrest each year for marijuana? Numbers such as these are misleading. To quote *Rolling Stone* magazine, also a proponent of legalized marijuana: "less than one percent" of federal and state inmates in our prisons and jails "are in for marijuana possession alone."[21] Here is how *Rolling Stone* breaks it down:

> About 750,000 people are arrested every year for marijuana offenses in the U.S. There's a lot of variation across states in what happens next. Not all arrests lead to prosecutions, and relatively few people prosecuted and convicted of simple possession end up in jail. Most are fined or are placed into community supervision. About 40,000 inmates of state and federal prison have a current conviction involving marijuana, and about half of them are in for marijuana offenses alone; most of these were involved in distribution.[22]

(*Rolling Stone* cites, and nearly quotes verbatim, the recent book *Marijuana Legalization: What Everyone Needs to Know*, by Jonathan P. Caulkins, Angela Hawken, Beau Kilmer, and Mark A. R. Kleiman.)

The argument that there are hundreds of thousands of arrests each year, though true, is unconvincing. There are over one million DUI arrests each year,[23] and over one million larceny-theft arrests each year,[24] but those sheer numbers tell us very little. They certainly do not tell us that we are losing the fight against intoxicated driving or the war against crime. What needs to be known about those numbers, as about the "arrested for marijuana" talking point, is threefold. First, is the action that is illegal worthy of being illegal, i.e., is it bad, a wrong, an evil, something that hurts individuals or society? Second, if it is a wrong, are we using appropriate resources to combat it? Third, are incidents of the illegal activity going up or down?

Nobody would claim that we arrest too many DUI drivers or thieves, even though we spend more money and effort doing just that than we do targeting marijuana distribution. So it is not the sheer number that should be the focus. It might be argued that the number should fit the crime. For example, if we directed more resources to jaywalking than drunk driving, that would be a mistake. Having highlighted the dangers of marijuana, we believe it should be illegal. The government not only has a right, but a duty to keep the public safe from harm, including dangerous substances. We struggle to imagine anyone who would rather the government not be in the business of regulating food, drugs, and any number of other commodities or products that are harmful or deadly. Does anyone really believe the use of asbestos in office buildings should be a right? Or that drug companies should not need to go through an FDA approval process with new pharmaceuticals? Or that physicians should not be licensed and regulated, and prohibited from performing quack procedures and making false promises?

So to the question of who is being arrested for marijuana-related crimes. It is simply and definitively not your seventeen-year-old son, smoking a single joint in the basement of your house. Nor is it his teacher, on summer break, smoking a joint while preparing an outdoor dinner for friends. Nor is it the friends at the dinner. Most are incarcerated for distribution, that is, drug dealing. Kevin Sabet, the former drug policy advisor in the Obama administration, wrote that "legalizing marijuana will not make even a small dent in America's state or federal imprisonment rates. That is because less than 0.3 percent of all state prison inmates are there for smoking marijuana...Moreover, most people arrested for marijuana use are cited with a ticket. Very few serve time behind bars unless it is in the context of another crime or a probation or parole violation."[25]

As the former director of the Office of National Drug Control Policy, John Walters, explained it during his tenure:

It is extremely rare for anyone, particularly first time offenders, to get sent to prison just for possessing a small amount of marijuana. In most states, possession of an ounce or less of pot is a misdemeanor offense, and some states have gone so far as to downgrade simple possession of marijuana to a civil offense akin to a traffic violation...

On the federal level, prosecutors focus largely on traffickers, kingpins, and other major drug criminals, so federal marijuana cases often involve hundreds of pounds of the drug. Cases involving smaller amounts are typically handled on the state level. This is part of the reason why hardly anyone ends up in federal prison for simple possession of marijuana.

He added,

Many inmates ultimately sentenced for marijuana possession were initially charged with more serious crimes but were able

to negotiate reduced charges or lighter sentences through plea
agreements with prosecutors.[26]

Michael P. Tremoglie is an author, journalist, and former Philadel-
phia police officer who recently dug into this "hundreds of thousands
of arrests" talking point of the legalization movement. His research
on his home state of Pennsylvania is worth quoting at some length.
Citing Pennsylvania Department of Corrections figures, Tremoglie
writes:

> According to the DOC, there are fewer than 300 people sen-
> tenced to prison in Pennsylvania each year for marijuana.
>
> Deputy press secretary, Susan Bensinger, furnished the
> following data: "There are about 256 sentences to DOC each
> year for marijuana. Only 5 of these 256 marijuana sentences
> to DOC are for possession of 'small amounts of marijuana.'
> Currently there are 13 inmates in DOC population whose con-
> trolling offense is 'possession of small amounts of marijuana.'
> Most (if not all) of these cases have other offenses (particularly
> DUI) in addition to the marijuana possession offense too."
>
> "Many people charged with the possession of marijuana
> do not spend one day in jail," said [Crawford County District
> Attorney Francis J.] Schultz.[27]

A 2010 Rand study put it graphically: "To provide a sense of
the intensity of enforcement, we calculated the risk a marijuana
user faces of being arrested for possession. If calculated per joint

consumed, the figure nationally is trivial—perhaps one arrest for every 11,000–12,000 joints."[28] (By the way, just how many joints are consumed nationally every year: 8.75 billion.[29]) Looking at California, the Rand study concluded that "most of those arrested for simple possession are not incarcerated at all."[30]

There are arrests involving marijuana, but rarely is there jail or prison time for simple possession. When there is an arrest for possession, it is usually of a large quantity—a lot of pounds (one Department of Justice study showed the median amount of marijuana seized in a possession arrest to be 115 pounds). Moreover, most of those in jail or prison for marijuana possession are there with other charges or have pled down from other charges.

Much the same is true in such law-and-order states as Arizona. As Yavapai County Attorney ("district attorney" in Arizona) Sheila Polk recently wrote, "Arizona does not lock up people for using marijuana. Our law prohibits incarceration until a third conviction, promoting, instead, treatment and drug courts."[31] It needs to be recognized that more than half of all drug treatment referrals come from the criminal justice system.

Legalization Will Not Put the Cartels Out of Business

When we do look at other marijuana arrests, they are for distribution or multiple convictions, not a weekend backyard barbeque with buddies having a college reunion. This takes us to the next myth argued by legalizers regarding distributors/dealers: that if we did legalize marijuana, it would put the violent Mexican cartels (some of the country's largest dealers, perhaps responsible for two-thirds of the marijuana sold in America)[32] out of business. The Mexican drug cartels have nearly ruined their country and now operate in dozens of American states and as many as three thousand American cities.[33]

It is laudable that we all want to be rid of them. Legalizing one of their products will not do it, though; in fact, it may fuel their efforts and revenue. As of now, cartels operating in Colorado are already trying to exploit new federal banking rules that have allowed for federally regulated banks to engage in business with marijuana dispensaries. At the same time, they are actively at work raising THC levels to become the preferred provider of recreational as well as medical marijuana.[34] Cartels are not solely in the drug business.[35] They have moved into other black markets, including prostitution, migrant smuggling, and the lucrative bootleg movie business. Does anyone argue it is a good idea to legalize bootlegged movies to help put cartels—and other bootleggers—out of business? Of course not, and least of all Hollywood.

We also have other data on the cartels and legalization. As one recent report put it, "the violent cartels could force their way in as black market wholesalers or simply rob pot dispensaries... but the general consensus is that the Mexican cartels will not quietly relinquish the Denver market. The owner of the Colorado Springs dispensary told the *Denver Post* he is planning to get a concealed-weapons permit for protection when he has to move money out of the store."[36] Now we have more guns combined with marijuana dispensaries. The truth we are seeing in Colorado is the truth we have seen in other cities that have relaxed their drug laws: where there are dispensaries, there is crime.

As Denver District Attorney Mitch Morrissey put it in 2013, the media is not doing a good enough job of showing the connection between medical marijuana and crime: "That is what I find most disturbing about this. Twelve people have lost their lives...And nobody is talking about it."[37] Tom Vigilante, a security expert who runs a private security company in Arizona, observed after a homicide at a medical marijuana dispensary in Tempe that dispensaries are always going to be targets. "They are a cash rich environment, not to mention a lot of environments with marijuana."[38] Or, as one veteran border narcotics agent put it, "Mexico is already in Colorado without the risks [meaning they can now more easily peddle a substance that used to be illegal]...Legal businesses will likely see a rise in extortion attempts while law enforcement will see a lot of backdoor deals being made."[39]

Moreover, the Rand Corporation has studied this very issue as it relates to the state of California, asking, Would legalizing marijuana in California reduce drug trafficking revenues and reduce violence in Mexico?[40] In a 2010 study, Rand scholars concluded, "not to any appreciable extent unless California exports drive Mexican marijuana out of the market in other states; if that happens, in the long run, possibly yes, but unlikely much in the short run."[41] California alone makes up one-seventh of America's drug market—more than any other state. Were it to fully legalize the drug, as Colorado and Washington State have, Rand concludes this would eat into, at most, about 3 percent of the Mexican drug cartels' profits.[42]

One other point about black markets and sumptuary laws: legalization does not eliminate black markets. As a recent report from the Tax Foundation has found, over 55 percent of the cigarette market in New York, over 50 percent of the cigarette market in Arizona, and nearly 50 percent of the cigarette markets in New Mexico and Washington are black market or smuggled cigarettes from other states.[43] What constitutes the black market smuggling of cigarettes? "Counterfeit state tax stamps, counterfeit versions of legitimate brands, hijacked trucks, or officials turning a blind eye."[44] The argument that legalizing and "taxing the heck" out of a product—as many legalizers argue for—will end the black market is simply not true.

Likewise, it is foolish to think that legalized marijuana will eliminate black market sales in Colorado. Recreational marijuana in that state is subject to a tax of 27.9 percent. This is comprised of a 15 percent excise tax imposed on the first transfer or sale from the cultivator to the retail marijuana store, a 10 percent state marijuana sales tax, and a 2.9 percent general state sales tax. There may be further local sales tax. This tax provides a strong incentive for marijuana consumers to purchase from the black market. It also motivates Colorado residents to obtain medical marijuana cards because that is subject only to the state tax of 2.9 percent. According to the Colorado Department of Public Health and Environment, rather than the anticipated decline in the number of medical marijuana card holders, in the first eight months since legalization on January 1, 2014, the state has received over 27,000 applications for new cards.[45]

The False Promise of Tax Revenues
for the States

One of the arguments in favor of full legalization has been that cash-strapped states would benefit from taxing the sales of marijuana. This, too, is false. As Sheila Polk puts it:

> Annually, there are three times as many alcohol-related arrests as marijuana [in Arizona]. Marijuana legalization does not mean fewer arrests. It means more charges for driving under the influence…child neglect; more drug-dependent newborn babies; and public disorder—putting it on par with alcohol.
>
> For every tax dollar collected from alcohol sales, 10 more are spent to address alcohol related criminal conduct, treatment, unemployment, and healthcare.[46]

Legalizing Marijuana Will Cost Society
Far More Than Tax Revenues
Will Generate

Here is the point: to those who claim alcohol is much more danger-ous than marijuana, and therefore that it is hypocritical to maintain the illegality of marijuana, we will see more damage and cost from putting marijuana on an availability par with alcohol. There is a reason alcohol use and abuse is more ubiquitous than marijuana use and abuse, after all: it is legal! The other point Polk raises brings up an interesting hypothetical. We do heavily tax alcohol and cigarettes. It would be interesting to ask governors what they would prefer, if they had the choice: keeping the tax revenue from alcohol and tobacco sales or eliminating the costs to their state associated with alcohol abuse and cigarette smoking. We surmise they overwhelmingly would choose the latter. The sumptuary revenues do not make up for the ancillary harms and costs. Kevin Sabet echoes Sheila Polk on this very point: "The $40 billion we collect annually from high levels of tobacco and alcohol use in the U.S. are about a tenth of what those use levels cost us in terms of lost productivity, premature illness, accidents and death."[47] The numbers on savings, budgets, and taxes never work out when it comes to taxing dangerous substances or substances subject to great abuse. The costs associated with just the Medicaid expenditures on behalf of those sickened by tobacco use run to about $22 billion per year. State and local tax revenues on tobacco, however, run to about $17 billion per year.[48] Many rightly observe that the costs associated with tobacco use run much higher than just Medicaid's numbers (think Medicare, private health insurance, and other unreimbursed costs). As for alcohol, it costs society upwards of $100 billion per year.[49] In stark contrast, combined state and local tax revenues on alcohol amount to just over $6 billion a year.[50]

Those are not the only costs, though. Too many at the human level simply cannot be estimated.

Dear Bill:

I'm 56 years old, and have been an active AA member for 24 years. I have a MBA and a BS in business. My IQ is 127. I started drinking at age 18, and soon afterwards starting using marijuana. Pot was definitely a gateway drug for me, as it led to many others, including LSD, cocaine, quaaludes, etc. By the time I graduated college at age 21, I was a full-blown addict. My life spiraled downhill until about age 32, when I quit drinking and drugs.

I've had trouble with relationships with women, and authority figures. I've been on antidepressants for about the last 20 years. I've had trouble keeping a job. However, I am a Catholic, and my spiritual life has become much bigger in my life in the last five years, so I'm doing better. But I can only imagine how much better my life would have been without alcohol and marijuana and subsequent drug use.

You could argue, I imagine, that because alcohol is legal, that my life still would be bad because of my alcoholism, but I think pot was a bigger problem for me. If I had pot, I was generally high—day or night. I believe marijuana is a very dangerous drug. It takes away any ambition, hopes, and dreams you have of a better life. It fries your brain. Thank you for your work in trying to bring this to light.

Jack in OH

It is true, Colorado has seen its tax revenues go up since marijuana has been taxed there. The estimates of tax revenue Colorado has taken in from January through July 2014 vary, from a low of about $12 million to a high of $21.8 million in marijuana tax revenue,[51] and more is, obviously, to be expected.[52] But whether the number is $12 million or $22 million, this is a far cry from what was predicted prior to the vote to legalize in Colorado—less by 46 percent *or more* from what was predicted, according to a report by the Pew Charitable Trusts.[53] Proponents are now saying we are getting more revenue and not any of the harm predicted. However, that is akin to saying a person in his first year of smoking is showing no harm to himself. No doctor, and nobody with an ounce of common sense, would accept that as an argument for the safety of cigarettes. Depression, psychosis, loss of teen motivation, and addiction do not happen overnight. This, among other reasons, is why Democratic Colorado Governor John Hickenlooper would forgo the revenue in his state. As he recently put it, "I hate Colorado having to be the experiment... We should not try to get people to do more of what is not a healthy thing."[54]

Actually, Prohibition Was Not a Failure

Finally, one cannot engage in the discussion of marijuana legalization without someone bringing up the era of Prohibition and what a dismal failure it was. That talking point does not fully match reality. None of us want to go back to the days of Prohibition, nor do we support illegalizing that which has been enjoyed for millennia.

However, if the main goal of Prohibition was to limit or reduce alcohol use and abuse in America, *that did in fact happen*. As the journalist Daniel Okrent found in his recent and comprehensive book on Prohibition, *Last Call*, Prohibition had the effect of reducing alcohol consumption by 70 percent in its first few years. Furthermore, the highest rate of consumption of alcohol in American history was 2.6 gallons of pure alcohol per person just before Prohibition. It stayed below that for a long time, even long after repeal, not reaching that level of 2.6 gallons again until 1973. Today it is 2.2 gallons per person.[55] Also, as Professor Mark Moore of Harvard's Kennedy School of Government has noted in a piece in the *New York Times*:

Cirrhosis death rates for men were 29.5 per 100,000 in 1911 and 10.7 in 1929. Admissions to state mental hospitals for psychosis declined from 10.1 per 100,000 in 1919 to 4.7 in 1929. Arrests for public drunkenness and disorderly conduct declined 50 percent between 1916 and 1922…[V]iolent crime did not increase dramatically during Prohibition. Homicide rates rose dramatically from 1900 to 1910 but remained roughly constant during Prohibition's 14 year rule. Organized crime may have become more visible and lurid during Prohibition, but it existed before and after.[56]

Prohibition had undesirable effects and consequences but two things are true: it did reduce consumption and resulting negative health and social consequences. Unlike our efforts to keep marijuana illegal, Prohibition was aimed at adults, whereas our primary concern today is children. As for the idea that the drug war has failed, and Prohibition-type policies have not worked with drugs, as we will see, this was not always true. We have reduced drug use in America in our lifetimes, but then we let up. The story and statistics are worth retelling, as they provide the guide for reducing use. It worked once, and it can again.

Chapter 5

How the Culture Once Successfully Fought Back on Substance Abuse

Following a chapter on myths, it is worth taking on one more: that we simply cannot win or make serious progress in "a," "the," or "any" war on drugs. As to whether the war on drugs is a "failure," as many—including Republicans and Democrats—often say, that is debatable. The annual budget of just the New York City Police Department is approximately $4.6 billion, more than half of what it costs the entire nation to enforce marijuana laws.[1] Yet there still is crime in New York City. Have the police or the efforts against crime failed? Or, rather, are they a necessary force for safety that costs money to maintain? Can and do they improve statistics over time? Yes, obviously efforts to reduce crime can succeed.

That a lot of money is spent while a problem continues is not seen as a sign of failure in almost any context other than drugs. We spend a lot of money on various government obligations in this country. Indeed, budgets go up almost every year in every government department from the local city to the federal government. Take your local US Attorney's office. That it still exists, that its budget increases every year, does not mean it is failing to do its job; it simply means it has a big job to do. Somehow the effort to fight against drug use and abuse is seen in a different light. The money spent is seen as an indication of failure simply because drug use and abuse continues in this country. We say that about almost nothing else we spend money on in America.

However, the question arises, can we do better? The answer is obviously yes, and the truth is that we once did better—much better—and not so long ago. The story of how we, as a society, did that and how we let up is both instructive and prescriptive, because to make major headway again would actually not take much money. It may, however, take something much more difficult to provide: a change of attitude, a change of thinking, both from our elected officials and from our cultural leaders and entertainers.

Today there are approximately twenty-five million users of illicit drugs.[2] Marijuana is the most frequently used of these drugs, with about nineteen million current users, and usage on a steady increase over the past several years.[3] These numbers, however, are not the worst they have been in our lifetimes. It is a handy premise of many that we cannot stop people from using illegal drugs. It is a convenient argument that we need to legalize them, but that is surrender.

It is surrender to murderous cartels, it is surrender to drug dealers, and it is surrendering our children to impaired, less productive, shortened, and possibly even disastrous lives.

We actually once did get drug use down in this country, to record low levels, because we took it seriously as a nation and as a culture. We are losing that sensibility today. The numbers prove it, as do some of the cultural messages being disseminated and, frankly, not being disseminated.

A Plan to Reduce Illicit Drug Use

In 1979 we reached the high-water mark of illicit drug use and abuse in this country, with over twenty-five million drug users (over twenty-three million of them marijuana users) in a population of about 225 million. By 1992 we'd reduced drug use in this country to its low-water mark, twelve million users; we more than halved the number. We had over 14 percent of our population abusing drugs thirty-five years ago. We got that number down to under 6 percent by 1992. In 1979 over 14 percent of those aged twelve to seventeen were regular users of marijuana. By 1992 that number had been reduced to 3.4 percent.[4] Today, that number is over 9 percent.[5] Over all ages, we have almost the same number of regular drug users today as we had at our high-water mark. This is the same number of Americans, the same number of souls addicted to drugs. We had gone from over 14 percent to fewer than 6 percent and are now creeping back up to 10 percent. See here:

Illegal Drug Use in America 1979 – 2009

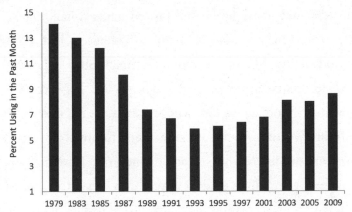

Source: Authors' reproduction based on Substance Abuse and Mental Health Services Administration Center for Behavioral Health Statistics and Quality, *National Survey on Drug Use and Health* (formerly the *National Household Survey on Drug Abuse*)

Looking at the effort from 1979 to 1992, an honest statistician or public policy expert would have to admit that a reduction of 50 percent or more is an enormous public policy success by any definition. In fact, it is hard to think of almost any other public or national policy effort in which we reduced any problem by that much. How did we achieve that and how did we lose it?

In the 1980s, the dangers of drug use became a national focus. That's how we tackled it. Today the harms of drug abuse are almost nowhere on the national radar screen. Quick questions: can anyone name the current drug czar? Can anyone tell us if there is a current drug czar? The inability to answer those questions tells most of the tale of the seriousness with which the government takes this issue and how the general media covers it.

When the drug issue does pop up, it fades quickly. Take a look at some of the national and international talents we have recently lost to substance abuse problems: just to name a handful, Whitney Houston, Michael Jackson, Amy Winehouse, Heath Ledger, Cory Monteith, and Philip Seymour Hoffman. Such unbelievable, remarkable, unique talents, wasted and now gone. For each of those six, how many more do we lose whose names are not known? How many future Whitney Houstons? How many future discoverers and geniuses and trailblazers in science or the arts? How many plain good citizens whose lives made a wrong turn, never to come back? It is true, marijuana was not the cause of the deaths of any of the above, but as we will see, marijuana was where most of their drug stories began. As one caller to my (Bill Bennett's) radio show put it recently and as we will document: "Not everyone who uses marijuana goes on to harder drugs, but nearly everyone who goes on to harder drugs started with marijuana."

Dear Bill:

My husband had two sons from his first marriage, one who became a high school math teacher and coach and who successfully raised a family in his one and only marriage. The other son, younger by five years, had lived for a longer period of time with his mother, who had lupus and was also an alcoholic/addict. For her younger son's 15th birthday, she gave him a case of beer and taught him how to smoke pot...and from then on, he slowly moved farther and farther into the same world as his mother. By the time I met him, he was 21 and in college, but not even close to graduation. He finally left college and started looking for jobs, but of course without a degree, little was available to him. He blew through several jobs before he went back to his mom's house, with the reason that she was very sick and needed his help to take care of her. After she died, he stayed there, and he did manage to clean up for a while, get a job and several promotions, got married, and fathered a beautiful baby girl. However, about three years into his marriage, when he was working as an assistant manager at a major truck stop, his boss discovered that money was missing from the safe. It turned out that my stepson was buying heroin with it. The company sent him to a detox center a couple of hundred miles away, where he lived for six weeks and seemed to do well, but it didn't take long for him to slide back into heroin use. He went back to detox, but left before finishing the whole course this time, and his wife told him not to come back home. He lived with us for a little while before taking off for an aunt's house (she had agreed to take him in under her very strict rules) in Arizona. He got a job in construction and soon moved to an apartment with one of his cousins...and all the drug behavior started all over again. Then suddenly, at age 32, he was found dead. It has never been clear if he shot himself or if his cousin shot him during an argument or what. His father and brother were devastated, and I was just horrified.

Age 32 . . . only 17 years since his mother had introduced
him to pot. Since then, I've never doubted that pot was
dangerous in itself or a gateway.

Marilynn in TX

We have seen a major cultural shift in attitudes toward drugs, especially marijuana. We have gone from being united in the 1980s and
early 1990s in recognizing the harm caused by drug use, to the culture of the late 1990s through today, in which drug use, or at least
marijuana use, is thought not to be harmful and sometimes thought
to be helpful. As the Monitoring the Future survey results on drug
use show, and as common sense would indicate, when perceived
risk falls, use increases. Kevin Sabet said it well: "Education about
the health dangers of marijuana use is the key to increasing perceived risk, just as prevention is key to lowering the long-term costs
to society of drug treatment. It has been estimated that for every
dollar we invest in drug use prevention efforts, up to ten dollars is
saved in treatment costs."[6]

Those old enough to remember will recall how much the cultural
message used to be anti-drug. There were the "This is your brain
on drugs" ads that were ubiquitous on television. There were sit-
coms aimed at children that featured anti-drug messages. President
George H. W. Bush and First Lady Nancy Reagan, in their tenures,
gave innumerable speeches on the harms of drug use. When I
(Bennett) was appointed the nation's drug czar, President George
H. W. Bush had the entire cabinet attend my swearing-in ceremony
to send a message. When President Obama's drug czar was sworn

in, not even the President attended; Vice President Joe Biden was left with the honor. That sent a message too, or a lack of one. That drug czar, Gil Kerlikowske, ultimately left, and the job was then held by an acting director, Michael Botticelli.

As I (Bennett) wrote several years ago, during the late 1980s, when we were serious as a nation about drug use, the news media also helped simply by giving intense coverage to the devastation wrought by drugs. People sitting in their living rooms were watching families and neighborhoods being ripped apart by drugs, and they began to pay attention.

One of the most encouraging signs of a strong cultural shift away from drug use occurred when I (Bennett) visited with Richard Frank, the president of Disney Studios. He asked me to address the Academy of Television Arts & Sciences when I was drug czar and the Academy responded, telling me there was a new "sobriety chic" in Hollywood, and that drug use was no longer "in." What I told Hollywood is a message we should be repeating again and again, not just to Hollywood (if we can), but also to friends, neighbors, and educators in the suburbs of America: your neighborhood may be stable and well situated. Its residents have resources of which they can take advantage. Many can afford expensive drug treatment programs that cost tens of thousands of dollars a month. Nonetheless, "For every Hollywood and Beverly Hills, there is a Watts. For every Chevy Chase, Maryland, there is an Anacostia. For every Scarsdale, there is a Harlem. We should not kid ourselves, often it is the wealthier communities that fuel the drug cartels' and dealers' businesses. That, after all, is where the money is."

Our warning was that the affluent should not become immune to the dangers in their own communities, nor to the struggles of the underclass who can least afford cycles of dependency and abuse. After all, Hollywood bore some responsibility for getting us into the drug mess by glorifying so much drug use in the 1970s. They were honorable in helping us get out in the mid- to late 1980s, when very few movies glorified drug use and some made strong anti-drug statements.

The culture of indifference to drugs (at best) and glorification of them (at worst) was put on the run, much as the culture of indifference to cigarette smoking was put on the run. Not so long ago, one could see Johnny Carson smoke on *The Tonight Show*. It was commonplace for actors to smoke on television, and for people to smoke in restaurants, on airplanes, and in their offices. Today one has to tune into *Mad Men*, a cable television show depicting New York City's Madison Avenue advertising industry in the 1960s, to see smoking on television. If one wants to smoke during business hours today, he or she has to walk outside, even in the cold sub-zero winters in the Midwest and on the East Coast, and often stay twenty or more feet away from the entrance of a building. One can no longer smoke in airplanes and only two airports in America even have smoking rooms. Indeed, some airports, Indianapolis as one example, ban smoking both inside and anywhere outside the airport. Smokers receive scowls and uninvited comments today. We even read movie reviews in major newspapers today that alert us, "Warning: Cigarette smoking depicted." We have not seen a review in a long time with a warning about the depiction of marijuana smoking or other drug use.

Our Culture Is Sending the Wrong Message

Sadly, the pendulum has swung in the exact opposite direction, and now marijuana smoking, far from being stigmatized like cigarette smoking, has been glamorized and even celebrated. Where once it was seen as cool to smoke cigarettes, it is now the height of uncool. Where once one would be thrown out of college for possessing marijuana, today the popular student is the one with the medical ID card.

What was one of the most popular television shows of this past decade, with a seven-year run, starring some of Hollywood's best talent (and still available on the Web)? A weekly show called *Weeds*. It was not about gardening. It was on the culturally hip Showtime.

Starring the highly talented and popular Mary-Louise Parker and featuring actors and actresses such as Kevin Nealon, Lee Majors, and Julie Bowen, *Weeds* was a very popular weekly drama/comedy about the life and times of a marijuana-growing and -dealing family headed by Parker's character. The show made light of marijuana culture, of marijuana growing, dealing, and smoking. While the audience was entertained by the fictional family Parker headed (as she kept the family afloat growing and selling marijuana), a few story lines from the show raised the eyebrows of those of us who do not think marijuana dealing and smoking are all that enjoyable or funny.

Parker's character, Nancy Botwin, dated a DEA agent who was ultimately killed in a drug bust she was responsible for. One of her teenage sons became a marijuana smoker and dealer. Her friends and brother-in-law got involved in her trade and became dealers and smugglers (of both marijuana and illegal aliens). She slept with practically every unrelated male character in the show. It was actually a pretty sad life when one took a step back and realized the sum and substance of the Botwin family existence, even as the comic portrayal resulted in audiences' rooting for her and her family's success in their escapades against law enforcement.

The point for the audience was to laugh and cheer for the Botwin family as they engaged in a lifestyle clouded in marijuana smoke. The tragedies mentioned above were glossed over as stumbling blocks they had to overcome along the way toward the family's ultimate success in its business.

Death, dropping out of school, sexual escapades, and addiction (not to mention occasional jail time) are, actually, a rather typical tale for those who succumb to a lifestyle of addiction and/or drug dealing. It is not a "success" that any family we know would choose. The DEA is in the way, the law is in the way, and conventions like school for teenagers are in the way—in the way of the Botwin family's "success," which it always seems to achieve. The audience is enticed to celebrate the Botwin family's overcoming the laws and conventions in their way. If you think our portrayal is a bit harsh or overstated, consider the show description from the head of Showtime, Robert Greenblatt: "Our ratings were va-va-va-voom! Who said hedonism is passé?"[7]

The problem of drug use and abuse has become, if not passé, something we have either turned a blind eye toward, become inured to, or—thanks to Hollywood—actually cheered on. Perversely, what we used to denounce, too many of us have come to accept, defend, and even positively support. Fifteen or twenty years ago, such a show would never have made it on air. As a nation and a culture, we took this issue seriously. Drugs, including marijuana, were not meant for laughs or to be celebrated.

Stigmatization and illegality are nearly gone for marijuana, and use has gone up—chronic use has in fact increased 84.3 percent since 2000.[8] In constant dollars, the money spent by Americans on marijuana went up from $21.6 billion in 2000 to $40.8 billion in 2010.[9] That is more than Americans spend each year on pornography, Halloween, and video games combined. Contrast that with the $8 billion spent on law enforcement against marijuana and tell us where the real waste is.

How can we reclaim the high ground in the cultural messages we deliver about marijuana? We can do it without raising a single penny in taxes. First, and most importantly, we must do it through education. Regrettably, most people are simply unaware of the dangers of marijuana or the increased potency of THC in today's marijuana, both of which we documented earlier. Let us bring back the ads detailing the dangers of marijuana, but with all the improved graphics and technology that are now at our disposal. Corporations interested in productivity and workplace safety have every reason to pay for these ads. Second, take a page from the huge advances our nation has made in addressing issues such as cigarette smoking, cancer, and other health and social problems. How did we do it? Everyone got involved; everyone from the top of our culture to the bottom, everyone from industry to politicians to Hollywood. Hollywood's charitable program Stand Up to Cancer provides a great example for other issues.

So how about a Stand Up Against Drug Abuse campaign? Captains of industry must help, but that includes Hollywood. Indeed, Hollywood buy-in is critical. We now have a large crop of actors and actresses who have damaged their lives and careers with drug use and abuse and miraculously got sober and stayed sober, and they never want to go back. Start with someone like Robert Downey Jr. He was the most promising actor of the 1980s, and then his drug abuse robbed him of a lot of life. It nearly ended his career as he was arrested again and again. Today he's been drug-free for at least ten years and told *Parade* magazine recently, "I used to be so convinced that happiness was the goal, yet all those years I was chasing after it, I was unhappy in the pursuit. Maybe the goal really should be a life that values honor, duty, good work, friends and family." Certainly this is not a bad ethic to teach to others.

The list of actors and entertainers who have been fortunate enough to overcome their addictions is a long one. Society has cheered for them and repaid them for their recovery at the box office. We think it would be a good idea to ask many of them to help deliver a national message to prevent others from going through what they did. Unfortunately, not everyone makes it. Those who do are the fortunate ones, and their luck can be rewarded. Let them be role models for what not to do. Let them testify to what it was like thinking they were going to die. Let them testify to waking up in a cold jail cell. Let them testify to the ruined relationships and the time they lost forever and wish they had back. And let them do it in a message that we see over and over again. Let's engage a national campaign with the likes of Beyoncé, Carrie Underwood, Reese Witherspoon, Anne Hathaway, Jennifer Lopez, Taylor Swift, Alan Jackson, the Williams sisters, Tom Brady, Jimmie Johnson, Danica Patrick, Brett Favre, and Russell Wilson. These are, of course, just examples. Include athletes, actors, and musicians who have not ever succumbed to drug use. We know how to do this—this issue has earned it.

Let us urge our leaders, our presidential candidates and Presidents, to get with the message, too. They are the best witnesses there are, and they are the most listened-to human beings on the planet right now. When the President speaks, it still means something in America, just as it does when he does not talk about an issue.

Then let us get to work on a national fund to fight marijuana medication and legalization initiatives in other states. The pro-marijuana lobby is very well funded and organized. The anti-marijuana advocates fight state by state, year by year. We do not need to invest in retracting and recalling initiatives where they have already passed. Our view is that the citizens in those states will see their folly in time and do that themselves. Instead, taking a page from Abraham Lincoln, let us stop legalization where it is and arrest its spread, putting its use, credibility, and abuse on the course toward ultimate extinction. Our cause will lead to a healthier, safer, more intelligent, and happier America.

There are not many public policy success stories of turning a tide in America once an ill has been normalized. It happens rarely, but we have seen it in race relations. We have seen it in reducing crime through better policing with innovative programs such as CompStat and the use of criminological theories similar to "broken windows."* We have seen it with cigarette smoking. We have seen it with drunk driving. In all, almost none of it required more public money than was already being spent. With the exception of crime reduction, most of it was attitudinal, achieved through education and messaging... and, ultimately, that was what helped lower crime too. Surely we can develop effective drug awareness education and messaging programs to effect a reduction in drug use. In other words, lowering substance abuse rates, like lowering crime, cigarette smoking, and drunk driving, is not about ability, it is about will. It is not about whether we can do it, it is about whether or not we will do it.

---

*CompStat and "broken windows" are a computer management tool and theory of policing, respectively, made famous by NYC Police Commissioner William Bratton, James Q. Wilson, and George Kelling in reducing crime in New York City—one a computer model used to fight crime based on neighborhoods and statistics, the other a philosophy of fighting crime in neighborhoods by starting with low-level misdemeanors and property damage.

Chapter 6

The International Experience

In almost every area of public and social policy, Americans will cite another country's policies and experience in support of their position. This is and has been true in everything from education reform, gun control laws, and the death penalty, to the sexual mores of our political leaders. It is no less true of the debate over drugs and, particularly, marijuana. However, frequently the examples from other countries are given incompletely or, worse, selectively.

Of course, very few serious social scientists believe that what one country does (especially on another continent) can be easily imported to another country, given vast differences in culture, family structure, socioeconomic factors, and other differences among populations. Rarely does a discussion of marijuana policy take place without someone's pointing to experiences in other countries, particularly the Netherlands or Portugal. While there is no shortage of argument regarding those countries' lax policies, we believe a more complete picture needs to be drawn. Experiences with those policies abroad have not, on closer examination, been all that benign. If anything, they are greater reason for caution.

Marijuana in the Netherlands

Take the Netherlands, for example. The conventional wisdom about that country is that marijuana is legal there and there are few problems... or at least fewer of the problems we in America have with addiction, teen abuse, and unjust incarceration. That conventional wisdom is almost all wrong. While the Netherlands may have some of the least restrictive marijuana laws in Europe, the substance still is not legal. Since the 1970s marijuana possession in the Netherlands has been illegal, but tolerated up to a point. The government prosecutes those who violate the toleration policy. That policy, literally called the "Policy of Tolerance," allows individuals over the age of eighteen to possess up to five grams of marijuana in public and thirty grams in private. One may not own more than five marijuana plants.[1]

Over the past two years, the Netherlands have tried to put that genie back in the bottle and backtrack on this "tolerance." Ironically, the Netherlands is backtracking on its lax marijuana policies just as we are liberalizing ours here in the United States. One problem is the number of "drug tourists" coming into the Netherlands to buy and smoke marijuana. It should be pointed out that it is not just those from other countries who have created problems in the Netherlands.

The claim that the Dutch marijuana laws have not affected the teen population there is demonstrably incorrect.

The THC levels of marijuana have increased in the Netherlands, as they have in the United States and elsewhere. The increased THC levels have wrought additional problems. There are now special rehabilitation clinics in the Netherlands, aimed at treating teen marijuana addiction. According to a 2009 survey, those centers have increased fourfold since 2002. As one youth worker told Radio Netherlands Worldwide:

Some of the problem cases smoked their first joint at age nine, in the school playground... The majority of cannabis users are taking the drug for a reason, as a sort of self-medication to fall asleep easily, to forget misery or quarrels in the family, or problems at school. It's no longer innocent. When those kids are received into the clinic, they are often suffering from psychosocial problems.[2]

Additionally, since 2011, the Dutch government has been working to classify higher-THC marijuana with other, harder drugs. According to the Economic Affairs Minister of the Netherlands, weed containing more than 15 percent of its main active chemical, THC, is so much stronger than what was common a generation ago that it should be considered a different drug entirely. The high potency weed has "played a role in increasing public health damage."[3]

The other canard about the Netherlands policy is that there is decreased use as a result of liberalized rules. It is simply untrue that the Netherlands has a far lower rate of use than the United States among its teen population. A 2010 Rand study found that "the U.S. rate exceeds the Dutch rate, but they are fairly close—indeed roughly equivalent within sampling and measurement error. Second, both the U.S. and the Netherlands rank high relative to most other nations."[4] In other words, while there is a teen marijuana use problem here in America, there is just about the same usage in the Netherlands. Moreover, there is more use or abuse in the Netherlands than there is in a range of other European countries, including, but not limited to, Norway, Sweden, Russia, Hungary, Poland, and Italy.[5] Finally, one other interesting note on the tolerance of the Netherlands from the Rand study: compared to other European nations, "Dutch students do indeed rank higher for lifetime prevalence of cannabis than for tobacco use, getting drunk, or use of other illicit drugs."[6]

As for the drug tourism problem the Netherlands created through their tolerance policy, it is both interesting and telling that one of the ways the Dutch are trying to crack down on it is by closing marijuana "coffee shops" that are deemed too close to the nation's schools. Were school-age use and abuse not a problem, this would not be a necessary solution any more than it would have been necessary to ban the use of Joe Camel in cigarette advertising, or to limit tobacco advertising to areas outside of school zones. The Netherlands are well ahead of the United States in understanding the pressure on children of nearby marketing of marijuana.

The Netherlands' new policy is national, but it is enforced at the local level. Thus, in Amsterdam, foreigners can still go to the marijuana "coffee shops," but Amsterdam has closed those shops near school campuses, and the mayor recently won court permission to close some twenty-six of the city's seventy-six "coffee shops" due to his concern over their confluence with the city's brothels (which he also is trying to close) and "crime."[7] The city of Maastricht is taking full advantage of the new, stricter laws, and not allowing noncitizens to purchase marijuana in the shops, many of which they also have closed.[8] Far from the Netherlands being an innocent experiment or a successful one, which actually reduced use, the latest United Nations report on international narcotics found that in the Netherlands, "illicit cannabis production has been estimated to be increasing since 2008, with the main destinations reported to be Germany, Italy, the United Kingdom and the Scandinavian countries."[9]

Drugs and Portugal

Portugal decriminalized personal drug use in 2001, and was the first country to officially do so. A long and interesting profile was done on Portugal and its experience with decriminalization in the *New Yorker* a decade later, in 2011. The reporter found that "serious drug use is down…the burden on the criminal justice system has eased; the number of people seeking treatment has grown."[10] The article lists other positives as well, such as a reduction in infectious diseases. However, is it an unambiguously good sign that more people are seeking treatment? Does this not indicate that more people are experiencing serious adverse consequences of drug use?

Ironically, the reporter for the *New Yorker* missed the main part of his own story, as he profiled one heroin addict ("Miranda") as an example of a beneficiary of the law. It is worth pointing out what the *New Yorker* finds a positive effect of the Portuguese law:

> With a stable family, a regular dealer, and his spot in the parking lot, Miranda's life has become orderly, almost routine. "This is because of the law," he said. "We are not hunted or scared or looked upon as criminals," he added, referring to the country's addicts. "And that has made it possible to live and to breathe." I asked if he had ever tried to overcome his addiction. He shrugged. "I guess I should," he said. "I know I should. But I'm not sure I can, and it isn't really necessary. I am lucky to live in a society that has accepted the fact that drugs and addiction are part of life."[11]

This, sadly, is the "positive," the "benefit" of decriminalization—"a regular dealer," in a society where "drugs and addiction are part of life," and with no incentive to believe it necessary to overcome his addiction. Of course, once a crime is decriminalized, there will be lower crime statistics. In the end, is it a success when drugs and addiction are a routine part of life? Not every expert in Portugal is on board with decriminalization, as the *New Yorker* profile is honest enough to reveal. A prominent director of a well-known rehab center in Lisbon says of Portugal's law decriminalizing drug possession and use, "This law takes away all pressure to stop using drugs...Nobody stops without pressure. That's not the way humans are built...[A]re we not simply creating a society that is completely socially dependent?" Countries, states, and cities that have decriminalized are often a tale of two or more countries, states, and cities. Portugal is, after all, not the be-all and end-all of perfection: as the 2013 crime report on Portugal by the US Department of State finds, "Portugal continues to see a gradual rise in a majority of its crime categories, including violent offenses." Beyond this experiment in Portugal, other European countries are finding problems, as they have with the Netherlands. The Department of State report further reveals an analogue to the problem Colorado has created for other states in America: "Portugal continues to be a gateway for drugs entering Europe, particularly from South America and western Africa."[12]

Not surprisingly, there is the war over statistics. For example, the most current study that proponents of Portugal's policy point to does show declining use of drugs, from marijuana to cocaine, in certain age groups. However, it seems conveniently to draw the line at arbitrary ages to achieve that statistical significance. For example, as a recent White House study on Portugal's drug policy and statistics found:

As "proof" of drug legalization's success, the [Cato] report trumpets a decline in the rate of illicit drug usage among 15- to 19-year-olds from 2001 to 2007, while ignoring increased rates in the 15-24 age group and an even greater increase in the 20-24 population over the same period."[13]

Additionally, the White House found the following:

> Statistics compiled by the European Monitoring Centre for Drugs and Drug Addiction (EMCDDA) indicate that between 2001 and 2007, lifetime prevalence rates for cannabis, cocaine, amphetamines, ecstasy, and LSD have risen for the Portuguese general population (ages 15-64) and for the 15-34 age group. Past-month prevalence figures show increases from 2001 to 2007 in cocaine and LSD use in the Portuguese general population as well as increases in cannabis, cocaine, and amphetamine use in the 15-34 age group. Drug-induced deaths, which decreased in Portugal from 369 in 1999 to 152 in 2003, climbed to 314 in 2007—a number significantly higher than the 280 deaths recorded when decriminalization started in 2001.[14]

These kinds of numbers led Dr. Manuel Pinto Coelho, President of the Association for a Drug Free Portugal, to say "Decriminalisation in Portugal was not a blessing. Decriminalisation didn't help us."[15]

Legalization of Marijuana in Uruguay

On this side of the Atlantic, the country American proponents of liberalized marijuana laws like to point to is Uruguay. Again, we restate our general reservation about attempting to import different countries' laws into America, based on a variety of differences.

As criminology professor Peter Reuter of the University of Maryland put it when asked about whether we should adopt the Portugal model, "Portugal is a small country and the cyclical nature of drug epidemics—which tends to occur no matter what policies are in place—may account for the declines in heroin use and deaths." The reality of Uruguay and its marijuana laws does not lead us to rethink our conclusions. If anything, it reinforces them.

At the end of 2013, Uruguay legalized the production, consumption, and sale of marijuana. As of this writing, it is too early to have many reliable statistics on how Uruguay (population 3.3 million) is faring with this experiment, but we do see several problems on the horizon. Our prediction is that things will unravel from optimism to regret in fairly short order.

First, one of the justifications for the law in Uruguay was to seek investment for the production and experimentation with medical marijuana and pharmaceutical companies. That hope seems to have been misplaced:

Uruguay's marijuana law has created a stir among some investors, including well known names in the medical marijuana industry in Canada and Europe... An executive of one medical marijuana producer, who asked that he and his company remain unnamed for regulatory reasons, said entrepreneurs had approached the company with the idea of working together in Uruguay. But he expressed concern that Uruguay is lumping recreational and medical cannabis under the same law, risking the reputations of medical marijuana research companies.[16]

Another concern is that, unlike in the Netherlands or Portugal, the new law in Uruguay does not make any provisions for treatment, or what has become known as "harm reduction." Raymond Yans, outgoing president of the United Nations' International Narcotics Control Board, has stated that the Uruguayan law, and debate leading up to it, have ignored "the scientific health problems related to marijuana" and that the new legislation "will not protect young people, but rather have the perverse effect of encouraging early experimentation, lowering the age of first use, and thus contributing to...earlier onset of addiction and other disorders."[17]

We shall see what becomes of Uruguay and the rest of South America as a result of its decision. Already Uruguay's neighbor to the north is worried. The president of Brazil voiced her concerns to the Uruguayan president, and Brazil is beginning "to step up its controls of people and luggage, should the predictions come true of rising numbers of passengers travelling to and from Uruguay."[18]

The Legalization Debate in Other Countries

Beyond those countries, other countries' experiences are relevant to the legalization debate, as well. France, the country most sophisticates point to in comparisons to the United States with its restrictive morals, has never legalized or decriminalized marijuana. This past year, for the first time in France's history, a member of parliament (from the Green Party) proposed a bill to legalize marijuana in France. Interestingly, that member of parliament took her cues from the United States, saying,

The fact that we proposed the law now is related to what's happening in the United States...If the law has changed in Washington and Colorado, we felt we had to open the debate now. Prohibition is useless.

And American President Barack Obama's statement that marijuana is not any more dangerous than alcohol, that also made us realize it's time.[19]

A French lawmaker proposed legalizing marijuana for the first time ever because of the American movement in that direction and comments made by the President of the United States. However, marijuana remains illegal in France.

Germany is a different story. While possessing and consuming marijuana is officially illegal in Germany, a "small amount" is tolerated. That amount varies by state or region in Germany.[20] Interesting to us is the German polling that shows over two-thirds of German citizens oppose the legalization of marijuana.[21] That is a much greater percentage than in America where, in most polls, the majority is now in favor of legalization.

Two countries that used to receive a lot of attention regarding their drug laws and problems, but are not discussed much anymore, are Singapore and Colombia. The drug laws in Singapore (where penalties for marijuana possession can range from caning to lifetime imprisonment) are, obviously, too draconian to ever even consider. Yet they do, in theory at least, prove one point...or disprove one: "you simply cannot successfully outlaw drugs." Yes, you can. Very tough laws on drugs and enforcement of those laws can and do lead to less drug use. In Singapore, 0.005 percent of the population uses marijuana.[22] Mexico is now seen in the same way we used to view Colombia. In the 1980s drug cartels practically ran and nearly ruined Colombia. At the time of drug kingpin Pablo Escobar's death, in 1993, the murder rate in Medellín was the highest in the world. Just last year Medellín registered its lowest murder rate in three decades.[23]

In many ways Colombia is not an apposite example, given that there are a great many differences between the United States and Colombia, and that the drug most at issue there in the eighties was cocaine. Still, there are some lessons to draw from the Colombia experience: when a society sees enough wreckage from drug dealers and abusers, it can indeed roll up its sleeves, take on an entrenched drug organization (or several), and reverse its course both politically and culturally. The US Special Forces, aiding the Colombia military, also were a critical player in Colombia's turnaround from a crime-ridden danger zone to which no sane American would ever travel, to a resort country to which travel and style magazines throughout America recommend vacations. Our main issue today is not cocaine, but marijuana. While we do not support the use of the US military to enforce our drug laws (except, in some cases, at the border), we do believe that when a country gets serious, it can reduce its drug habit.

While today Mexico is not a failed state, it certainly is close. It is legal to carry up to five grams of marijuana in Mexico, and anything more is illegal. There is no medical marijuana law in Mexico either. Even the liberal president of Mexico, Enrique Peña Nieto, remains opposed to legalization, or did until now. Recently President Peña Nieto told Reuters: "I repeat, I'm not in favor of legalization, this is a personal conviction. But we can't continue on this road of inconsistency between the legalization we've had in some places, particularly in the most important consumer market, the United States, and in Mexico where we continue to criminalize production of marijuana." Peña Nieto is being pressured to follow the United States's—particularly Washington's and Colorado's—lead. He states in the interview that it is ultimately impossible for the United States and Mexico to have different drug laws. He is correct.

We have discussed how further legalization in the United States will not radically diminish the work of the drug cartels operating in Mexico or the United States. Indeed, there has been zero decline in black market marijuana growth and production in Colorado by drug trafficking organizations (DTOs) since the state legalized the drug.[24] The DTOs still control roughly 65 percent of the black market marijuana operations in the US forests of Colorado.[25]

Some point out that the cartels in Mexico are no longer planting as much marijuana as they used to because of the recent years of legalization in the United States, but they are not exactly letting their land sit fallow. They are replacing their marijuana with poppies to supply the United States with more heroin.[26] The unfortunate truth about the cartels is that they are now vastly sophisticated corporate networks involved in all kinds of black markets for both legal and illegal substances, including coal, limes, avocados, and bootlegged movies.[27] It is interesting that we have yet to hear anyone in Hollywood suggest that we decriminalize the bootlegging of movies in order to starve the cartels of the millions of dollars they make on that black market. What Mexico needs is a Colombia moment, wherein brave citizens, communities, and armies say, "Enough!" and take their country back. Instead it is getting encouragement to go in the other direction—that of making the illegal legal—from, of all places, the United States.

Great Britain's Experience with Marijuana Liberalization

The UK is a study in misjudging the consequences of lowering the category of offense for marijuana possession, while marijuana growers are at the same time raising its potency. It is also a study in how difficult it is to put the decriminalization and legalization genie (or smoke) back into the bottle.

Great Britain has tried to reverse course after lowering the criminal classification of marijuana. An editorial from 2007 in London's center-left *Independent* newspaper took a stance in favor of lowering Britain's classification of marijuana, but experience changed its view. Titled "Cannabis: An Apology," its article said in part,

> In 1997, this newspaper launched a campaign to decriminalise the drug. If only we had known then what we can reveal today.
>
> Record numbers of teenagers are requiring drug treatment as a result of smoking skunk, the highly potent cannabis strain that is 25 times stronger than resin sold a decade ago.

More than 22,000 people were treated last year for cannabis addiction—and almost half of those affected were under 18. With doctors and drugs experts warning that skunk can be as damaging as cocaine and heroin, leading to mental health problems and psychosis for thousands of teenagers, *The Independent* on Sunday has today reversed its landmark campaign for cannabis use to be decriminalised...

The editorial continues:

Professor Colin Blakemore, chief of the Medical Research Council, who backed our original campaign for cannabis to be decriminalised, has also reconsidered.

He said: "The link between cannabis and psychosis is quite clear now; it wasn't 10 years ago."

Many medical specialists agree that the debate has changed. Robin Murray, professor of psychiatry at London's Institute of Psychiatry, estimates that at least 25,000 of the 250,000 schizophrenics in the UK could have avoided the illness if they had not used cannabis... "Society has seriously underestimated how dangerous cannabis really is," said Professor Neil McKeganey, from Glasgow University's Centre for Drug Misuse Research. [28]

As the editorial makes clear, efforts to decriminalize marijuana can result in harms that cause many to rethink their earlier support for it.

The UN Is Concerned About US Violations of Drug Control Conventions

Despite a generalized relaxing of drug restrictions and enforcement throughout the world, the latest report from the United Nations describes growing international drug problems. A few selections:

In Africa, there has been a sizeable increase in the trafficking of opiates through East Africa and cocaine in North and East Africa, as well as a sizeable increase in the illicit manufacture and trafficking of methamphetamine in the region; abuse of opioids, cannabis, amphetamine-type stimulants and cocaine is also increasing.

Central America and the Caribbean continue to be affected by drug trafficking and high levels of drug-related violence. The region remains a significant transit route for cocaine destined for North America and Europe. Large-scale illicit methamphetamine manufacture is a cause for serious concern.

Unprecedented numbers and varieties of new psychoactive substances have been reported in Europe, and their abuse continues to grow.

Methamphetamine manufacture appears to be spreading to new locations in Europe.[29]

The United Nations' International Narcotics Control Board is unhappy with the United States: "Use of cannabis in some states of the United States of America has not yet been adequately addressed by the federal Government in a manner consistent with the provisions of the drug control Conventions."[30] In other words, while the UN is trying to battle drug abuse and the failure of states throughout the world to eliminate narcotics and trafficking, the United States, rather than showing the way, is undermining the effort. In the meantime, looking at Colorado's medical marijuana experiment, the United Nations report found: "Emerging data from the State of Colorado of the United States suggest that since the introduction of a widely commercialized 'medical' cannabis programme (poorly implemented and not in conformity with the 1961 Convention), car accidents involving drivers testing positive for cannabis, adolescent cannabis-related treatment admissions and drug tests revealing cannabis use have all increased."[31]

In sum, it is simply incorrect to say the national or international tide of laxity in enforcing marijuana laws, be it through decriminalization or legalization, has been met with unbridled success or, for that matter, approval by the experts. If anything, the mature judgment has been, and is, to rethink such policies. We predict Uruguay will soon find that out, too.

Chapter 7

How to Answer Legalization
Efforts and Argue with Those
Who Support Legalization

Over the last year, one could have looked at almost any poll on the legalization of marijuana and, for the first time, find that support for legalization has become the majority sentiment in this country. A CNN poll from January 2014, for instance, found 55 percent of the population in support of legalizing marijuana.[1] That is a greater percentage than voted for President Obama in either 2008 or 2012. In years past, such a number would have raised eyebrows and voices. Historically, Americans understood the dangers of drug use and would never have been in favor of legalizing it. In 1987 only 16 percent of Americans supported marijuana legalization. By 1996 that number had risen to

26 percent and it has been rising ever since, to a strong majority of Americans.²

We have attempted to explain some of this. As a society, we stopped the drumbeat against the harms of drugs (including marijuana). We watched a slow and steady campaign that actually moved from saying marijuana was not harmful to trumpeting marijuana as beneficial, despite scientific evidence that grows by the day. Even as we were writing this book, two major studies came out on the dangers of marijuana: one study on its effects on the brain, another on harms to the heart. As we noted earlier, we can find no peer-reviewed study from the past several decades that actually finds marijuana safe or healthy. Let us repeat: we have found no serious scientific or medical study that concludes marijuana use is actually safe or healthy. Every argument on behalf of its safety or therapeutic value is based on anecdote or political argument... or a critique of a study on the harms of marijuana, where the dissenting conclusions about such studies come down to something very much like, "The study is overstating the danger."

The anecdotes, political arguments, and disagreements with the scientific research have been buffeted and strengthened by cultural messages, to the point that most polls now show that we live in a country where most people want to legalize a dangerous drug. It is our suspicion that a great many people still do not actually believe it is a good idea to legalize marijuana, but have been cowed into silence or resigned agreement by the tide of the movement to legalize. Regrettably, those who do still suspect legalization may not be a good idea, or have inclinations against it, often do not have good arguments to respond to the changing culture and politics of the time. It is our purpose to supply those arguments. As Flannery O'Connor put it, sometimes you must "push back against the age as hard as it pushes against you."[3]

So how does one begin the conversation or debate against legalization? It depends what the first argument in favor of legalization is, and we have tried to answer the most common ones here. Let us break it down as simply, comprehensively, and helpfully as we can.

The Science Documenting the Harms from Marijuana Use Is Clear

First, there are no scientific or medical studies showing marijuana is safe or harmless. The best the legalization advocates can do is cast doubt on studies showing the opposite, mostly by critiquing methodologies. To critique such studies is to critique every study, including those from respected institutes in Europe and the United States, as well as almost every physician and health organization, including the American Medical Association, the American Psychiatric Association, and the American Cancer Society. In fact, it is inexplicable that as the balance of public opinion has been moving toward the legalization of marijuana, the balance of science and medicine has been moving toward broad agreement on marijuana's harms and dangers. Ask a proponent of legalization who says marijuana is not that harmful, "Do you have a study on that?" Then you might show them one of the studies we have referenced regarding the very real dangers to the heart, brain, and lungs.

Is Marijuana Really Less Harmful Than Alcohol or Tobacco?

The most widespread argument we hear in favor of legalization is that alcohol and tobacco are legal substances that do far more harm to individuals and society than marijuana. However, even if alcohol and tobacco were more harmful than marijuana, is it hypocritical to keep marijuana illegal because there are more harmful substances that are legal? We think not. Adding another dangerous product to the marketplace defies sound judgment.

We believe that marijuana is at least as harmful as tobacco and alcohol. Someone can smoke a tobacco cigarette, or drink a can of beer or a glass of wine, and return to work, able to function at full capacity. The same cannot be said for someone who smokes a marijuana joint during the lunch break, since the sole purpose is to get high. Certainly, if someone smokes two packs of cigarettes or consumes six scotches on the rocks per day, there will be very negative consequences. However, someone does not need to engage in such excessive consumption of marijuana to suffer both immediate and long-term negative consequences. Whenever marijuana legalization advocates talk about the dangers of alcohol and tobacco use, they are really talking about abusive use of those drugs. They then compare the alcohol and tobacco abusers to the pot smoker who has a joint once or twice a month. It is a false comparison. In assessing the relative harm caused by tobacco, alcohol, and marijuana, we need to be consistent and compare the harm done by abusive versus casual use of each drug.

It is simply untrue that tobacco is more harmful than marijuana. Yes, cigarettes can do terrible damage to the lungs, larynx, esophagus, tongue, heart, and other parts of the body. However, aside from temporary and fairly safe mental stimulation, they have no effect on the brain, except to cause nicotine addiction. Marijuana, on the other hand, affects the lungs, heart, and brain. Marijuana smoking is "significantly associated with more than a twofold risk of developing lung cancer" according to one recent forty-year cohort study.[4] The American College of Physicians documented in a report that "the chronic effects of smoked marijuana are of much greater concern, as its gas and tar phases contain many of the same compounds as tobacco smoke. Chronic use of smoked marijuana is associated with increased risk of cancer, lung damage, bacterial pneumonia, and poor pregnancy outcomes."[5] That is exactly what is said in lay terms about tobacco smoking.

As for the heart, one recent study from Harvard Medical School has found marijuana smokers increase their risk of heart attack five times over that of nonsmokers.[6] Another recent study, out this year and mentioned earlier, found that marijuana users are more subject not only to heart attacks, but also to "angina, ischemic ulcers and gangrene associated with blocked blood flow to extremities and transient ischemic attacks."[7] This research is complemented by another 2014 study finding "that marijuana users have a higher risk of stroke compared with people who do not use the drug."[8] Again, this sounds to the layman like warnings heard about cigarettes.

Then there is the brain. As the *Psychiatric Times* put it, "Results from 7 cohort studies showed a 40% increased risk of psychosis in cannabis users compared with nonusers. The data also revealed a dose-response effect—the risk of psychotic symptoms was increased approximately 50% to 200% in those who used cannabis frequently compared with nonusers."[9] Marijuana use has also been found to substantially lower IQ[10] and to cause and worsen depression and anxiety disorders.[11]

Marijuana Can Become Addictive

Regarding marijuana's being addictive, as Dr. Wes Boyd of Harvard Medical School put it, for some people "marijuana is unquestionably addictive."[12] Dr. Boyd explains that some people's experiences with marijuana are analogous to those who abuse alcohol: for some it is addictive, though most are casual users. Fair enough; most people who drink alcohol are not alcoholics. Alcohol addiction rates range from about 10 to 15 percent of users.[13] Nobody would maintain, though, that alcohol cannot be or is not addicting. What are the chances of addiction to marijuana? For teens it's one in six; for adults it's one in eleven.[14] So yes, it is true that the majority of people who try marijuana will not become addicted. However, that also is true of alcohol and tobacco and, for that matter, cocaine. In other words, it is not an argument at all to say most users do not become addicted. Nobody would make that claim about alcohol or tobacco as an argument for fewer restrictions on those substances.

As for the higher death and damage rates attributed to alcohol and tobacco, it is *at present* correct to say more deaths are caused by those two legal substances than by marijuana. It is also true that alcohol and tobacco are far more widely used because they are legal. About 136 million Americans age twelve and older drink alcohol; about 58 million Americans age twelve and older smoke cigarettes; and about nineteen million Americans age twelve and older are current users of marijuana.[15] However, note that marijuana use has steadily risen over the past several years (from about 14.5 million users seven years ago), and that even though alcohol is legal for those over twenty-one and illegal for those under twenty-one, still some 25 percent of sixteen- and seventeen-year-olds and some 46 percent of those eighteen to twenty are current drinkers of alcohol; and even though cigarettes are legal for those over eighteen and illegal for those under eighteen, some 8.6 percent of those under eighteen smoke cigarettes.[16] Why would anyone think the story of marijuana would be different? The argument that one can legalize a substance for only a certain age group is fallacious, and it has not been true of alcohol or tobacco. It is certain that legalization of marijuana will lead to more young people smoking marijuana. As Yavapai County Attorney Sheila Polk estimated, if Arizona legalized marijuana for recreational use along the lines of Colorado or Washington, thirty-two thousand more high school students in Arizona would smoke marijuana.[17] In Colorado, where marijuana was legalized in

January 2014 for recreational use for those over twenty-one, this
report came out to too little notice:

> While many Coloradoans rang in the new year by lining up out-
> side marijuana dispensaries for a celebratory toke, some rehab
> centers are prepping for an increase of marijuana-addicted
> patients in 2014, *especially teenage users.* [Emphasis supplied.]
> Although only people over the age of 21 are allowed to buy
> marijuana, psychiatrists and others remain concerned that
> teens could be most at risk for becoming addicted.
>
> Dr. Christian Thurstone, a professor of psychiatry at the
> University of Colorado and the head of the teen rehab center
> Adolescent STEP: Substance Abuse Treatment Education &
> Prevention Program, said 95 percent of patient referrals to the
> program are for marijuana use.
>
> After the law legalizing marijuana in Colorado passed in
> November, he started applying for a series of grants to expand
> his staff. He now has doubled his staff and still has a waiting
> list of patients.[18]

In a very short time, and despite program expansion, there developed a waiting list of teen patients seeking treatment for marijuana
addiction.

For those who say, "Let's experiment in a state or two and see,"
the experiment has been tried, and the evidence is already coming
in. How many more teens do we need to become marijuana addicts,
how many more dropouts do we need, how many more psychosis

patients do we want? How many more teens do we want moving on to even harder drugs?

Marijuana Can Lead to Use of Harder Drugs

This gets us to whether marijuana is a gateway drug. There is great debate on the question "Does marijuana lead to harder drugs?" We have tried to point out that marijuana itself, especially with ever-increasing THC levels, is a pretty hard drug as it stands. It is harmful and dangerous enough that the gateway argument should almost be academic, but it is not. It is real, and the effect has had real-life consequences, or perhaps we should say real-death consequences.

Dear Bill:

Marijuana certainly was a gateway drug for my nephew. His parents divorced when he was around 10. His father was/is a drug abuser and had spent time in prison. My nephew started smoking pot when he got a job at age 14 at a movie theater. From that point on he progressed to other drugs. By the time he was in high school he couldn't go to school, he was snorting cocaine. His mother thought it was a phase he would get through and never took the drug abuse seriously. My Mother and I tried desperately to talk sense into my sister's head with no results. By the time my nephew was 22 yrs old he had been doing heroin for almost a year. He was a dealer from his mother's condo while she went to work at a judge's office. Everyone in the condo area knew what was happening except for my sister (clueless). Within that year of heroin use he tried rehab but felt he was not like "those other people," called his mother, and she brought him home. A few months later my nephew was dead from an overdose of heroin in the condo where he and my sister, his mother, lived.

This has caused so much grief for our entire families and for the grandmother (my mother) that for the last three years since his death I have spoken to my sister only a couple of times. Only recently she speaks to our mother. My sister will not admit any mistakes; she has stated that his death has "taught her so many things about life" and that she wouldn't take back one moment of what has happened. My own two children who are now 21 and 24 are adamantly against drug use; they know it is a ticket to nowhere and that death or prison may await you one day—as it did their cousin.

Connie in PA

Recall the list of famous actors and musicians who recently died from drug overdoses that we mentioned earlier? Heath Ledger started with marijuana.[19] Whitney Houston started with marijuana.[20] Cory Monteith started with marijuana.[21] Amy Winehouse started with marijuana.[22] Kevin Sabet, echoing that radio caller we mentioned earlier, put it this way: "Although most people who use marijuana will not go on to use other drugs, it is indisputable that users of illegal drugs other than marijuana almost always begin with marijuana."[23] Study after study confirms this statement.

Dear Dr. Bennett:

My family's experience: Our two daughters started smoking pot in middle school (1990's) via the kids in school, both dropped out in the 9th grade. Then upgraded to Crack followed by ecstasy, meth/crank and then Oxycontin (Oxy) and any other pill they could find. Their husbands would grow in the spare bedrooms pot to smoke and sell to afford the Oxy and meth, adjacent to their children's rooms.

My wife and I are educated small business owners, we never expected any of this nor do we have the knowledge or training to provide mental health for two drug addicted sociopaths, we have come to realize. It occurred to me lately that these new ultra high THC level marijuana breeds or what the kids refer to as (KB) Killbud mixed with any other narcotic is altering the children's minds in such a destructive way the consequences are irreparable.

Family summary

3 daughters have 5 children in our family (My wife and two sisters)

Three of the children started smoking Marijuana, all moved to any drug they could find and none can hold a job or be permitted at family gatherings due to violent behavior problems.

Two of the children are doing very well.

Of 5 grandchildren who lived in the POT smoking households, all need psychological help today.

After 23 years of fighting this battle and losing we broke all contact "Tough love" as the last weapon left in our arsenal.

So far so good is not a phrase I can ever use in this situation.

With Respect!

Phillip in FL

What we already know is that as the brain, especially the teen brain, gets accustomed to the marijuana high, it requires more and more of the drug to obtain the same or better effects. More or stronger marijuana will be sought. Not surprisingly, other drugs will also be sought to increase the high or better affect the pleasure centers of the brain. Additionally, we know that marijuana users tend to have more social interaction with peers who use marijuana and other drugs. Social acceptance of wide drug use by one's peers may well contribute to acceptance of one's own broader drug experimentation and use. Where there are other drugs, there is usually marijuana— as was found in Michael Jackson's bedroom, and as was found at Philip Seymour Hoffman's heroin dealer's home.[24]

Marijuana need not lead one to other, harder drugs to be dangerous, though certain evidence points in that direction. A recent study out of the Yale School of Medicine found that 34 percent of those abusing prescription medications had previously used marijuana.[25]

Other studies have revealed, as the *Journal of the American Medical Association* reported, "that marijuana-using twins were four times more likely than their siblings to use cocaine and crack cocaine, and five times more likely to use hallucinogens such as LSD." Another study found that 62 percent of the adults who first tried marijuana before they were fifteen were likely to go on to use cocaine. In contrast, only 1 percent of adults (or fewer) who never tried marijuana used heroin or cocaine.[26]

Do we really want to gamble with the future of our children by assuming that all these findings are overstated? Whatever the detractors have to say about the gateway effect of marijuana, we do not want the focus to be taken off the harms of marijuana itself. That is the point here. Despite what we indisputably know about marijuana, many refuse to accept it, or turn a blind eye. While any scientific study will have its detractors and cause debate, there is little to no debate about the fact that marijuana has a negative effect on the brain. No one person can seriously say marijuana use makes him or her more intelligent, more articulate, a better driver or operator of equipment, or more sober in judgment. Though it may help as an analgesic, as does almost any other well-known illegal drug (or alcohol), unquestionably it still has negative health consequences.

Hence the modern-day irony: we are at a crucial time in our nation's history, engaged in a debate over a national health care system, and still struggling to improve schools whose graduates are behind their peers in many industrialized nations. The great education desiderata within the Democratic Party today is more funding for more early education programs. It is entirely inconsistent to be fighting for these programs at the same time that we mainstream the use of a substance that leads to poor academic performance, dropping out of school, and lower IQ. Similarly, we are at odds when we try to "bend the health care cost curve down," as the phrase goes, while relaxing strictures on or encouraging the use of a substance that causes ED admissions, the need for treatment programs, and other negative consequences.

There is another modern-day cultural irony, as well. In 2014, when the drugstore chain CVS announced it would no longer sell tobacco products, its CEO stated, "Cigarettes have no place in an environment where health care is being delivered."[27] Health care advocates and many others lauded that bold move, even hoping other pharmacies and drugstores would follow suit. Walgreens, in fact, stated it would study the issue after CVS's announcement.[28] Knowing that marijuana cigarettes contain many of the same carcinogenic substances and organic and nonorganic compounds as tobacco, that inhaling smoke is unhealthy, and that marijuana affects judgment and can lead to brain abnormalities, how can it be that we are expanding the availability of marijuana at the same time that we are celebrating the lack of availability of cigarettes? Why are cities and states cracking down on the use of trans fats and sugar products for teens and adults at the same time that they are facilitating greater marijuana availability?

Let us make no mistake about it, and even the proponents of legalization will admit this: legality leads to availability. Availability leads to and encourages far more use. Ethan Nadelmann, founder of the pro-legalization Drug Policy Alliance, admits more people in their "40s, 50s, 60s, 70s, 80s, and 90s" will start using more marijuana if it is legalized.[29] He claims young people will not because they already have access to it. His point makes little sense. If young people have access to it, so do older people. Young people have access to it because they obtain it from older people. Just recently two fourth graders were caught selling marijuana at their elementary school in Colorado. They got it from their grandparents.[30] As the Rand study we cited earlier found: legalization in California would cut the price of marijuana by as much as 80 percent and increase use by anywhere from 50 to 100 percent.[31]

Alcohol and Tobacco Are Harmful, So Why Would We Want to Make Another Harmful Drug More Available?

This takes us to the last point in the argument over alcohol, tobacco, and marijuana. Having clarified the premises of the argument that marijuana is not harmful, or not as harmful as alcohol or tobacco, let us assume the premise is right. Almost everybody would concede marijuana has some negative health consequences. Now imagine three bars in a graph. One is the quantifiable damage to individuals and society caused by alcohol. The second is the quantifiable damage to individuals and society caused by tobacco. The third is the quantifiable damage to individuals and society caused by marijuana. For the sake of analysis, let us concede the third bar is the shortest. Now, legalize marijuana. How will those bars be affected? Will alcohol damage go down? Will tobacco damage go down? Or will marijuana damage go up? The question answers itself and the point is this: legalizing another substance will not reduce the negative consequences of substances that are already legal. It will simply add one more product to the marketplace of damage done to individuals and society. If anything, the argument that alcohol and tobacco are more dangerous than marijuana suggests that we should further restrict or make illegal alcohol and tobacco, not make legal something else that is already damaging, as well. After all, as the prescription drug abuse problem has worsened, has alcohol or tobacco abuse receded? No. This is why Joe Califano calls us "a high society." Once substance abuse becomes normalized, more substance abuse will take place. Once one substance is tolerated, society moves on to and will experiment with another.

Here is one further point about the studies we have referenced attesting to the dangers of marijuana. There is hardly a single study in social science that does not raise a debate within the field about its conclusions or methodology. There will be analysts who poke holes in all kinds of research. This is true of research on anything from crime reduction procedures to measuring intelligence to the surveys on political candidates for office. It is true of market analysis and it is true of automobile safety projections. It is true of predictions about gas prices and it is true of every form of medical research. It is also true of studies of marijuana and its effects on everything from the brain to the lungs. But here is the ultimate question about marijuana research: is half of it true? Is 10 percent of it true? Is any of it possibly true?

Taking the most skeptical view: if it is possibly true that marijuana use can lead to psychosis, if it is possibly true that marijuana use can lead to lung damage, if it is possibly true that marijuana use can lower IQ, if it is possibly true that marijuana use can lead to cardiac problems, why would society gamble with it? What responsible parent would hear a physician say, "Your child could benefit from using marijuana but you should know, there are some studies that show marijuana can cause psychosis, lung damage, heart problems, and permanent damage to your child's brain," and disregard those warnings? Even if none of this were true, we know marijuana is an intoxicant that more and more youth are using. At the most common sense level, with all the challenges we face from alcohol, tobacco, and other legal substances that end up in the hands of children, does it make sense to make available one more? It simply is not a good idea, indeed it is morally criminal, to facilitate inebriation and harm over sobriety and health.

States' Rights and the Libertarians

Now let's address the states' rights and libertarian arguments. Oddly, we find an agreement between left and right in America on this: when it comes to marijuana, many on the left of the political spectrum advance the states' rights argument, though they do not believe in states' rights on almost any other issue. Recently, Republican California Congressman Dana Rohrabacher penned an op-ed for the *National Review* titled, "Let States Decide on Pot."[32] Congressman Rohrabacher admits, "More studies tell us of serious psychological and physiological effects, such as a marijuana-induced tendency toward schizophrenia. But how is that not also the case with any number of prescribed or over-the-counter medicines now required to display voluminous safety warnings on their packaging?"[33] That is a wrong implied conclusion. The better questions are, "Are you happy with what citizens in America are doing with prescription and over-the-counter medicines? Has the availability of those legal substances not caused an increase in their abuse?" Of course it has. Search the Internet for the phrase "prescription drugs epidemic." About 1,810,000 pages is what Google turns up.[34]

Now let us take up the gravamen of Congressman Rohrabacher's article: "Call me a hopeless Friedmanite [follower of Milton Friedman], but I am convinced a freer market will work out safety standards and a way to publicize them. Why wouldn't it? Ultimately, individuals do hold their fates in their own hands; legal deterrence always falls short."[35] Does it? Does legal deterrence fall short in anything? Or does it just fall short of 100 percent compliance? As stated earlier, burglary is illegal, we spend a lot of money as a society preventing it, and it still happens. This does not lead us to the conclusion that we should spend less money and effort trying to prevent it. There would be more burglary if we did. The same can be said of almost any other crime—state or federal—that we can think of.

The essence of the states' rights and libertarian arguments boils down to this: it should not be the government's business to regulate what people want to do with their own bodies or safety. Of course most do not accept such an argument when it comes to building safety codes, child safety seats, or seat belts and airbags in their own cars. Bodily safety has frequently met the test of being necessarily the province of government enforcement. So, too, have drugs and medicine—at least since the beginning of the last century with the passage of the Pure Food and Drug Act, which tried to stamp out snake oil and the non-uniform processing, manufacturing, and peddling of "drugs" with little, no, or dangerous value.[36] With marijuana use, we seem to take a holiday from the understanding that a product can be marketed and actually be harmful—even when it is labeled as therapeutic or medicinal. Unlike most other things that the government regulates for safety purposes, drugs like marijuana are *not* the province of just one individual making a decision for him- or herself. Nor are they the province of one state. As Supreme Court Justice and states' rights proponent Antonin Scalia put it, "Drugs like marijuana are fungible commodities... Marijuana that is grown at home and possessed for personal use is never more than an instant from the interstate market and this is so whether or not the possession is for medicinal use or lawful use under the laws of a particular State."[37] This is precisely why we see Colorado adolescents in addiction rehab facilities: because of marijuana they obtained from adults who first obtained marijuana from a legal dispensary. This is precisely why we see adolescents from other states in addiction rehab facilities, having obtained marijuana whose point of sale was in Colorado.

Of course, as citizens of the United States who love their Constitution, we are all for states' rights and less government intrusion into the lives of all Americans. We support a state's right to make policy determinations for its citizens, but it is not a state's right to engage in a policy decision that renders a nullity another state's determination on the same or a similar policy. That is the true nullification at play here. As discussed earlier, Romneycare affected only the citizens of Massachusetts. Marijuana legalization and "medical marijuana" are having negative impacts on other states that have chosen not to legalize marijuana. As reported by the Rocky Mountain High Intensity Drug Trafficking Area in 2012:

- In 2012 there were 274 Colorado interdiction seizures of marijuana destined for other states, compared to fifty-four in 2005. This is a 407 percent increase.

- Of the 274 seizures in 2012, thirty-seven different states had been destined to receive marijuana from Colorado. The most common destinations were Kansas (thirty-seven), Missouri (thirty), Illinois (twenty-two), Texas (eighteen), Wisconsin (eighteen), Florida (sixteen), and Nebraska (thirteen). There were some seizures in which the destination state was unknown.

- From 2009 to 2012, compared to 2005 to 2008, the average number of interdiction seizures per year involving Colorado marijuana more than quadrupled from 52.2 to 242.1.

- From 2009 to 2012, compared to 2005 to 2008, the total average number of pounds of Colorado marijuana seized from interdictions increased by 77 percent from an average of 2,220 pounds to 3,937.

• In 2012, 7,008 pounds of Colorado marijuana that were destined for other states in the country were seized by interdictions.[38]

If California were to enact a policy that negatively affected Arizona or Nevada, California could not very well claim it had a state's right to enact that policy, any more than a homeowner can turn his house into a 24/7 party club that bothers the neighbors and maintain it is his personal, private property right to do so—especially when that choice is in conflict with the federal law. Oliver Wendell Holmes's notion that a person's right to swing his arm ends at another person's nose used to be a common sense recognition of rights and liberties, state and personal. Unfortunately, marijuana has changed that. States that do not want it are robbed of their choice to keep marijuana illegal—their state's right—by those that want to legalize marijuana. Those that do cannot escape the argument that their decisions have at least some negative effects. In other words, the states that accept "medical marijuana" or recreational marijuana must admit, just as the *National Review* editors admit, that with legalized marijuana, "Colorado's legal drug dealers inevitably will end up supplying black markets in neighboring prohibition states." So much for the rights of states that want none of this, or as little of it as possible.

There is one point that needs to be made about states' rights—it is invoked by those on both sides of the political aisle *when it is a convenient argument* for them. Conservatives, for example, who usually speak the most forcefully about states' rights, may not do so when the issue is the outlawing of certain abortion procedures. Even the greatest of conservative states' rights advocates, Congressman, and former Republican presidential candidate, Ron Paul voted for the federal ban on partial birth abortions, even though Congressional authority for the ban was based on the Commerce Clause. Congressman Paul did argue he had philosophical problems with his vote, but in the end, he did vote for the ban because he said it would have "the *possibility* of saving innocent human life" (emphasis supplied).[39] Even for Dr. Paul, "the possibility" of saving innocent human life and health was a legitimate primary concern trumping states' rights.

On the liberal side, rarely do we find arguments on behalf of states' rights outside of the issue of marijuana—we do not find them with regard to illegal immigration or abortion rights or nearly anything else we can think of. Those liberals that do claim to support a state's right to legalize marijuana rarely support a state's autonomy on any other issue (as but one example, see how aggressive the battle against Arizona's right to curb illegal immigration has been). As we say, the argument is usually one of convenience—and it does not have a very good legacy, invoked most frequently, as it has been in the past two centuries by Southern Democrats, on behalf of states to avoid and void civil rights laws.

What of the libertarian argument that adults should be able to decide for themselves what they wish to consume and what they want to avoid? There are huge economic and social costs that will be borne by everyone, not just the consumer. These include increased health care and treatment costs, lost productivity and absenteeism, work-related accidents, drugged-driving injuries and deaths, and the painful effects of addiction on family members. Each of these costs implicate interstate concerns and federal monies. As we already know, alcohol certainly has substantially contributed to added costs in each of these categories, and tobacco contributes greatly to health care costs. While we may never be able to fully reverse the burdens imposed on society by alcohol and tobacco users, that is hardly a reason to heap on significantly more costs by legalizing marijuana so that some people can indulge their high in the name of freedom.

All of this gets us to the major point of the libertarian and states' rights argument: What is the ultimate right being argued for? What is the philosophical price of not granting it? Outside of the limited medical usage that may need to be met, and which can have a federal protocol, at the end of the day the right is, simply put, a right to get and be stoned. This, it seems to us, is a rather ridiculous right upon which to charge a hill. If the right is not granted, after all, what is truly lost? Now ask yourself, if the right is granted, given the expanded adult and adolescent use of marijuana that will result from further legalization, what will be gained...or truly lost? In other words, were Americans really less free, were Coloradans less free, in 2001 or 2013 (the years before medical marijuana and recreational marijuana were fully implemented)? And have the costs—higher rates of use, higher rates of vehicular fatalities where cannabis was present, greater expulsion and suspension rate—of that freedom since then been worth it?

Our view is perhaps best summarized by Professor Jonathan

Caulkins in *Marijuana Legalization: What Everyone Needs to Know*. He wrote:

> About half of all days of marijuana use come from people who self-report enough use-related problems to meet criteria for substance abuse or dependence with respect to marijuana or another substance. Does the happiness a controlled user derives from using marijuana on a typical day offset the unhappiness of someone else spending a day harmed by and/or struggling to control problem drug use? In my opinion, the answer is no. In a free society there are plenty of other ways to have fun without insisting on a right to use something that becomes a stumbling block for others.[40]

His conclusion?

> I generally agree with the libertarian notions of letting people harm themselves if that's what they choose: but only to a point. I also believe people can be fooled; we are heuristic decision makers, not mechanical optimizers. Certain products and activities fool a sizable minority of us. For those special cases, I think the majority who would use responsibly ought to be willing to give up their fun to protect the minority who would not.[41]

Ultimately, however, not even this is the main point on states' rights and marijuana. The main point is logic. There is not a single logical argument on behalf of a state's regulating or deciding for itself the legality of marijuana that is not also true of cocaine, heroin, or prescription drugs. If a state has the right to regulate marijuana, why does it not have the right to decide for itself how to regulate—or even *whether* to regulate—cocaine? Or, for that matter, Oxycontin? Furthermore, it simply is a fallacy, as we have seen with Colorado and her neighboring states, to believe that one state can legalize marijuana without its having an effect on other states. Colorado's recreational marijuana, as well as medicinal marijuana, is regularly sold to people from other states and found in other states; and Colorado's neighboring state sheriffs are pulling over and arresting more and more drugged drivers coming out of Colorado. What Colorado does with respect to marijuana does not stay in Colorado. The same is true of every other state. At the end of the day, there is no logical or rational state's right to create its own drug policy—not when the field of law is preempted by federal legislation. There truly can be either one set of laws on drugs or fifty. We have yet to find a doctor or a US Attorney who thinks it a good idea for there to be fifty regulatory regimes for drugs.

Chapter 8
Conclusion

Our country is now moving in two directions on marijuana: at the very time that study after study comes out revealing the dangers of marijuana use, public opinion is moving further down the road of legalization. However, it is not just public opinion that has changed, it is the media as well.

In July of 2014, the *New York Times* editorial board saw fit to write a major house editorial calling for the legalization of marijuana. Its arguments were not that different from arguments on the right—from the likes of the *National Review* or congressmen like Dana Rohrabacher. As we've pointed out, marijuana erases a lot of traditional political distinctions. It unites Barney Frank with Ron Paul and the *New York Times* with the *National Review.*

In its house editorial "Repeal Prohibition, Again" of July 27, the editors at the *Times* not only ignored modern science and research, they ignored the recent writing of their longest-standing op-ed contributor, Maureen Dowd.

Interesting to us is that the *Times* has spilled no shortage of ink decrying the dangers of sugar and sugar beverages, especially for our youth, or the dangers of tobacco use and advertising to our nation's children; nor has it failed to note the importance of expending more money on early childhood education programs, because of the importance of our youths' brain development and of closing our nation's educational achievement gaps.

But none of those previous concerns were taken seriously in the promotion of the legalization of marijuana by the *Times*. The *Times* made several claims that are simply contradicted by arguments the editors have made in the past about the health of our nation's youth with regard to other products or policies, and it raised outdated red herrings in its characterization of those who would disagree with their position. Indeed, as we pointed out earlier, the outcome of such legalization would be far more dangerous than sugar beverages to our youth, and would reverse almost every gain efforts at better early childhood education could produce.

The *Times* cited a seemingly alarming number of arrests of those who have possessed marijuana. Arrests, however, do not tell the story. What is the conviction and incarceration rate for mere marijuana possession? In fact, it is very low. Recall what the pro-legalization publication *Rolling Stone* magazine wrote: "Not all [marijuana] arrests lead to prosecutions, and relatively few people prosecuted and convicted of simple possession end up in jail … [of those that do,] most of these were involved in distribution. Less than one percent are in for possession alone."

But what of the fact that a large number of people are arrested? Is there any crime committed in America for which the number of violators leads to the argument that the law should be dispensed with? Or, rather, does the number of violators lead one to the argument that enforcement of the law should be stronger? Think of almost any crime in America, and the answer is usually the latter. For marijuana, though, its supporters go in a different direction.

The *Times* then tried to bolster its case by citing the racial disparities in these arrests. Again, with almost any other crime, would anyone make the argument that because there is a disparity in who is arrested, the law should be done away with? Or, rather, does the disparity not lead one to argue for more even enforcement, i.e., targeting all communities the same way? If a good many non-minorities are breaking the law, any law, target them more, and we advocate that absolutely, but do not let up on enforcement simply because one group is getting away with what another group is not. Would the *Times* argue for dispensing with bank fraud or insider-trading laws simply because one group (white men in white collars) is disproportionately arrested for breaking them? Of course not.

The greatest offense to common sense and modern science came when the editors wrote:

There is honest debate among scientists about the health effects of marijuana, but we believe that the evidence is overwhelming that addiction and dependence are relatively minor problems, especially compared with alcohol and tobacco. Moderate use of marijuana does not appear to pose a risk for otherwise healthy adults. Claims that marijuana is a gateway to more dangerous drugs are as fanciful as the "Reefer Madness" images of murder, rape and suicide.

There are legitimate concerns about marijuana on the development of adolescent brains. For that reason, we advocate the prohibition of sales to people under 21.

Addiction and dependence are not relatively minor problems for adults or for children who use marijuana. Indeed, over 4.4 million Americans aged twelve and older meet the clinical criteria of the American Psychiatric Association for marijuana dependence or abuse, according to Department of Health and Human Services survey results.[1] In their book on drugs and drug policy, Professors Kleiman, Caulkins, and Hawken stated that:

Full legalization would involve both increased availability, as in the Netherlands, and also much lower prices. If the likely price effect on consumption is about threefold, and we add in some additional growth due to increased availability and decreased stigma and personal risk (such as arrest and the loss of employment) for users, we might expect something like four to six times as much cannabis to be consumed after legalization as is consumed now.[2]

Assuming the same proportion of dependents or abusers to users as is currently known, we should expect sixteen million to twenty-four million dependents or abusers. Of course these are estimates and the numbers could be lower, but given the trend of availability, decreased stigma, and decreased sense of harm, the numbers could be much higher, too!

Meanwhile, the comparison to addiction to and dependence on other dangerous products is no excuse to make society suffer even more. Does the *Times* think asbestos should be legalized and used to build college campus dorms as an educational cost-saving measure for families because, after all, more college students are harmed by binge drinking (with a legal but regulated product) than ever would be by asbestos inhalation? Or perhaps we could save money on eldercare by allowing nursing homes to use asbestos because more of their patients will die from Alzheimer's than late-onset lung cancer or COPD? Adding to the catalog of unhealthy products in America does nothing to reduce problems we already have; it only serves to increase the harm by adding yet another dangerous substance to the marketplace.

As for moderate use of marijuana not appearing to pose a risk for adults, why did the *Times* not consult its own pages and employees? Would "nibbling...a bite or two" of a candy bar made with marijuana constitute "moderate use"? That's what Maureen Dowd wrote about having done the very previous month—and the result? "I felt a scary shudder go through my body and brain. I barely made it from the desk to the bed, where I lay curled up in a hallucinatory state for the next eight hours. I was thirsty but couldn't move to get water. Or even turn off the lights...I strained to remember where I was or even what I was wearing...I became convinced that I had died and no one was telling me." We would argue it is pretty "risky" for an adult to think she has died and to be unable to summon the will or strength to get a glass of water.

Then, of course, our side is labeled with having the mind-set of *Reefer Madness* by the *Times* as well as others. When will the legalizers enter the new century? *Reefer Madness* is a movie from the 1930s, predating World War II. It is outdated and irrelevant to the discussion of marijuana today. How about a slightly newer television show? Perhaps *Weeds*, the Showtime series, would be more apt. This is the story of a fictional marijuana-selling family that works with cartels and kills off competitors as well as federal agents.

Let's acknowledge that today's marijuana is at least five times stronger than the marijuana of the past. The THC levels of today's marijuana average around 15 percent, but go as high as 20 percent and above in the dispensaries found throughout the states that have legalized it for "medicinal" or recreational use. The marijuana of today is simply not the same drug it was in the sixties, seventies, or eighties, much less the 1930s. It is much more potent, leading to a great many more health risks. Undoubtedly Maureen Dowd would not have written about the same experience, if she had sampled what marijuana used to be.

Finally, the *Times* makes the legitimate point that marijuana does, in fact, negatively affect the adolescent brain. Yes, it certainly does. As we've demonstrated, study after study has come out over the past ten years showing links between marijuana use and psychosis, as well as decreases in IQ in the teen marijuana-using population. These are permanent decreases, indicating permanent brain damage. Now, can the *Times* tell us of one substance—be it tobacco, alcohol, or prescription drugs—for which age restrictions have worked to keep that substance out of the hands of those below the prescribed age? Teens use alcohol and tobacco in such large numbers precisely because they are legal products. More marijuana is used now because its status has been changed from something that is dangerous and forbidden to something considered "medicinal" and even recreational in four states. It is a substance whose dangers the President of the United States recently downplayed, in the face of the very evidence his own Office of National Drug Control Policy, DEA, and National Institute on Drug Abuse promulgate.

It is ironic that less than three months after its editorial calling for the legalization of marijuana, the *Times* published an article in the Education section by Abigail Sullivan Moore, which is entitled, "This Is Your Brain on Drugs." As we have done in this book, her piece cites several recent studies documenting the harm smoking marijuana does to the brain and body, particularly in teens and young adults. In discussing the very negative impact that smoking marijuana has on college students, she quotes Dr. Breiter from Northwestern University, who said, "If I were to design a substance that is bad for college students, it would be marijuana."[3] Apparently, the editorial board of the *Times* was dismissive of this medical science regarding the serious threat posed by marijuana when it elected to advocate legalization.

It was the stigma and illegality of marijuana that kept its usage levels below those of cigarettes and alcohol. That will change ever more as the legality of marijuana becomes more widespread and its use becomes less stigmatized. Legality is the mother of availability, and availability, as former health, education, and welfare secretary Joe Califano recently put it, is the mother of use. As the *New York Times* reported only two months before its legalization editorial, regarding the state of Colorado: "Hospital officials say they are treating growing numbers of children and adults sickened by potent doses of edible marijuana."[4]

Our general point has been this: there are two conversations about marijuana taking place in this country. One, we fear, comes from an old understanding of low-THC marijuana that doesn't exist anymore; the other takes seriously the science of the new marijuana and its effect on the teen as well as the adult brain. If one truly cares about our public health, one needs to recognize the dangers inherent in the higher THC content of today's marijuana.

Beyond left and right, though, it is critical in terms of public, health, and legal policy to understand that there is such a thing as legal havoc, just as there are such things as personal, familial, and cultural havoc. The juggernaut of the movement to decriminalize, medicalize, and legalize marijuana in America is creating havoc in every possible category. To borrow from Abraham Lincoln, it wrecks and renders everything it touches. A recent Associated Press report from Colorado notes that "the legalization of marijuana has contributed to an increase in the number of younger people living on the city's streets."[5] Homeless people with felony backgrounds are now moving into Denver in an effort to work in the pot industry.[6]

In addition to neighborhood and street havoc, we are just beginning to see a crop of new legal problems, as well. Marijuana dispensaries are now challenging the appropriateness of being taxed, because they don't wish to admit that they are breaking federal law. If they declare taxable income from the sale of marijuana, they argue they would be self-incriminating by admitting to a violation of federal drug law. This is occurring just as proponents of legalization argue that tax revenues would enrich state coffers. Meanwhile the US Attorney General refuses to enforce federal marijuana law, sowing confusion among US Attorneys about what to do. Former Drug Czar John Walters has pointed out that we may soon start seeing civil lawsuits against dealers for marketing and selling dangerous and addictive products. The tort bar could, indeed, become even wealthier.

In the end, though, the havoc we see most—in too many of our daily lives, in our families' lives, and in our friends' lives—is that done to children and families. In January, the *Atlantic* published an article under the pseudonym "Leah Allen." It was titled, "My Dad Will Never Stop Smoking Pot." She couldn't have summed up better what we see too frequently. In the article she writes of how her father's marijuana addiction affected her family while she was growing up. Here's how she opened:

There's a lot of discussion about pot right now, as different states push towards legalizing it for medical or personal use.

As I listen to the various arguments—about health, morality, criminal justice, personal freedom—they all come back to the same thing for me: Dad, Dad, Daddy. The family element is almost always missing from the debates: What does smoking pot do, not only to users but to their children?

...[F]ear came most palpably for us while my dad was driving. He was likely to get distracted by other cars, by songs on the radio, or, in later years, by photos on his phone, sometimes turning his attention completely away from the wheel. NIDA notes that marijuana more than doubles a driver's risk of being in an accident. Many of our road trips ended early with broken-down cars left on the side of the road. On good days, my dad would forget to fill them with gas or change the oil. On bad days, he would nudge into something and a tire would go.

I don't know when my dad started to smoke. I do know that before he smokes a joint he can get antsy, angry. His temper is fast and sharp. He hit my mom when she was pregnant and that's when she left him. I was three. I also know that after he smokes, my dad is relaxed, soothed, likely to go off on dreamy tangents about colors and pictures.[7]

Ms. Allen continues about how her father would often forget her brother, sister, and her when he took them to events; he forgot birthdays and dinners. Her brother became addicted to marijuana at age twelve and dropped out of school, and now lives with their dad. Her sister also is now a marijuana smoker. While Ms. Allen's policy prescriptions do not make sense to us, she does conclude her article this way: "My dad will never stop smoking pot. Sometimes I wonder about the man he might have been, and the lives we all might have had, if he'd never started."

Any parent of a child who becomes dependent on marijuana can empathize with Ms. Allen, as can any grown child of a parent who is dependent. The devastation that befalls families that succumb to substance abuse is long. It is tragic, and it is avoidable, but only if we urgently take this issue seriously. Two of the strongest disincentives to initiate smoking marijuana have been taken away from adolescents. In times past, poll after poll would show that children who did not smoke marijuana said their reasons were that it was illegal, and that it was dangerous or unhealthy. Society has changed that, and the perceived harms of marijuana, especially among young people, are at an all-time low. Usage is creeping up to an all-time high.

While society has deemed unhealthy such products as cigarettes, sugar, and trans fats, marijuana is proliferating in legality and use. So too are its negative effects, from more drugged driving to more treatment admissions to more ER visits. Additionally, studies from respected medical journals and schools of medicine come out several times a year pointing to new research on the dangers of marijuana, be it to the brain, heart, or lungs.

How this happened can be summed up by a look at the cultural and political shift that began in the mid-1990s, when leaders and politicians stopped speaking of the harms of marijuana. When anti-drug ads became less prevalent, when arguments on behalf of marijuana use were no longer answered, when a market was found to create medical marijuana and call marijuana medicine because of its analgesic effects, and when Hollywood made punch lines out of the use of marijuana in blockbuster movies and popular television shows: that is when the public became much more accepting of the use of marijuana.

To families who struggle with addiction, marijuana is anything but funny, and it is not medicinal. We understand there are people with cancer or AIDS who are in great pain, suffering terribly, and who need strong relief or an appetite enhancer. We would deny almost nothing to them. They are, however, an extremely small percentage of those who get medical marijuana recommendations. As previously discussed, Arizona's distribution of medical marijuana cards indicates that only 3.76 percent of cardholders use marijuana to ease the symptoms of cancer. Another 1.53 percent suffer from glaucoma, while 1.06 percent have AIDS. These numbers are similar in other medical marijuana states where statistics are available. In the meantime, more and more marijuana from these dispensaries is ending up in the hands of adolescents, supplied by adults who have medical marijuana cards.

We anticipate that the states that have legalized recreational use will regret it, as have residents of cities across America, such as Mendocino County, Baltimore, and Anchorage. Even the residents of the Netherlands are now regretting their loose marijuana laws. Likewise, residents of Great Britain are lamenting the lowering of the criminal classification of marijuana.

We need not engage in scare tactics that have plagued the drug debate ever since the movie *Reefer Madness* came out in 1936. We simply ask readers to do their own research and not blindly accept the arguments on behalf of marijuana legalization or medicalization without some critical thinking and common sense. Almost every argument on behalf of legalization has a better countervailing argument. We have tried to make those here. It is not because we are invested in any financial outcome, as some who promote marijuana legalization are; it is because we are invested in the safety of our children and the strength and productivity of our nation. We urge those states still considering legalization or medicalization to look at what is happening in places like Colorado and ask if that is what they want for themselves—more use, more harm, more treatment. We do not believe the numbers will improve there, but that they instead will become dramatically worse. As Dr. Christian Thurstone at the University of Colorado said when asked, "When will we know if things in Colorado are getting worse?" "They already have."

William Shakespeare has Edgar in *King Lear* say: "The worst is not/So long as we can say 'This is the worst.'" If nothing else in this book worries our readers about the consequences of the legalization of marijuana, hopefully this prediction from marijuana research expert Professor Jonathan Caulkins of Carnegie Mellon University will influence their thinking about the ongoing debate: "My best guess is that legalizing marijuana would only double, or perhaps triple, abuse and dependence, from 4 to 8 or even 12 million people in the United States."[8] How many of these millions of substance abusers/dependents will be adolescents, since we know that the factors that most influence adolescent use of drugs, including marijuana, are availability, price, and perceived risk/stigmatization? Legalization will make all these barriers easier to surmount, whether full legalization or the back door of medical marijuana. Who will be held accountable for the many lost to abuse and dependence?

We would like to leave it up to the states that have embarked on these dangerous experiments to come to terms with what they have unleashed. We stand ready to help them in any way we can to reverse their decisions. But in the meantime, our main goal is to stop the juggernaut of legalization. We believe that with the argument now joined, sunlight will be the greatest disinfectant. We hope that there will be a larger national debate about the legalization of marijuana, whether medical or recreational. The discussion should be informed both by public awareness of the higher potency of today's marijuana and by the ever-increasing body of scientific evidence documenting the many adverse consequences of smoking marijuana. This argument is, after all, about our most precious and valuable assets: the health and well-being of our children and our country.

Appendix

Attached is an article reprinted with permission from the June 2014 *New England Journal of Medicine*, written by Drs. Nora Volkow, Ruben Baler, Wilson Compton, and Susan Weiss of the National Institute on Drug Abuse. It sets out a compelling and well-documented description of the known adverse health effects of marijuana use. Also included are letters to the editors of the journal by medical researchers from France to California, pointing to additional adverse health effects of using marijuana that they have researched. As the letters to the editors demonstrate, our knowledge about the full negative effects of smoking marijuana is expanding rapidly.

REVIEW ARTICLE

Dan L. Longo, M.D., *Editor*

Adverse Health Effects of Marijuana Use

Nora D. Volkow, M.D., Ruben D. Baler, Ph.D., Wilson M. Compton, M.D.,
and Susan R.B. Weiss, Ph.D.

IN LIGHT OF THE RAPIDLY SHIFTING LANDSCAPE REGARDING THE LEGALIZA-
tion of marijuana for medical and recreational purposes, patients may be more
likely to ask physicians about its potential adverse and beneficial effects on
health. The popular notion seems to be that marijuana is a harmless pleasure, access to which should not be regulated or considered illegal. Currently, marijuana is
the most commonly used "illicit" drug in the United States, with about 12% of
people 12 years of age or older reporting use in the past year and particularly high
rates of use among young people.[1] The most common route of administration is
inhalation. The greenish-gray shredded leaves and flowers of the *Cannabis sativa*
plant are smoked (along with stems and seeds) in cigarettes, cigars, pipes, water
pipes, or "blunts" (marijuana rolled in the tobacco-leaf wrapper from a cigar).
Hashish is a related product created from the resin of marijuana flowers and is
usually smoked (by itself or in a mixture with tobacco) but can be ingested orally.
Marijuana can also be used to brew tea, and its oil-based extract can be mixed into
food products.

The regular use of marijuana during adolescence is of particular concern, since
use by this age group is associated with an increased likelihood of deleterious
consequences[2] (Table 1). Although multiple studies have reported detrimental effects, others have not, and the question of whether marijuana is harmful remains
the subject of heated debate. Here we review the current state of the science related to the adverse health effects of the recreational use of marijuana, focusing
on those areas for which the evidence is strongest.

From the National Institute on Drug
Abuse, National Institutes of Health,
Bethesda, MD. Address reprint requests
to Dr. Volkow at the National Institute
on Drug Abuse, 6001 Executive Blvd.,
Rm. 5274, Bethesda, MD 20892, or at
nvolkow@nida.nih.gov.

N Engl J Med 2014;370:2219-27.
DOI: 10.1056/NEJMra1402309
Copyright © 2014 Massachusetts Medical Society.

ADVERSE EFFECTS

RISK OF ADDICTION

Despite some contentious discussions regarding the addictiveness of marijuana,
the evidence clearly indicates that long-term marijuana use can lead to addiction.
Indeed, approximately 9% of those who experiment with marijuana will become
addicted[3] (according to the criteria for dependence in the *Diagnostic and Statistical
Manual of Mental Disorders*, 4th edition [DSM-IV]). The number goes up to about 1 in
6 among those who start using marijuana as teenagers and to 25 to 50% among
those who smoke marijuana daily.[4] According to the 2012 National Survey on Drug
Use and Health, an estimated 2.7 million people 12 years of age and older met the
DSM-IV criteria for dependence on marijuana, and 5.1 million people met the criteria for dependence on any illicit drug[1] (8.6 million met the criteria for dependence
on alcohol[1]). There is also recognition of a bona fide cannabis withdrawal syndrome[5] (with symptoms that include irritability, sleeping difficulties, dysphoria,
craving, and anxiety), which makes cessation difficult and contributes to relapse.
Marijuana use by adolescents is particularly troublesome. Adolescents' increased
vulnerability to adverse long-term outcomes from marijuana use is probably related

Table 1. Adverse Effects of Short-Term Use and Long-Term or Heavy Use of Marijuana.

Effects of short-term use

Impaired short-term memory, making it difficult to learn and to retain information

Impaired motor coordination, interfering with driving skills and increasing the risk of injuries

Altered judgment, increasing the risk of sexual behaviors that facilitate the transmission of sexually transmitted diseases

In high doses, paranoia and psychosis

Effects of long-term or heavy use

Addiction (in about 9% of users overall, 17% of those who begin use in adolescence, and 25 to 50% of those who are daily users)*

Altered brain development*

Poor educational outcome, with increased likelihood of dropping out of school*

Cognitive impairment, with lower IQ among those who were frequent users during adolescence*

Diminished life satisfaction and achievement (determined on the basis of subjective and objective measures as compared with such ratings in the general population)*

Symptoms of chronic bronchitis

Increased risk of chronic psychosis disorders (including schizophrenia) in persons with a predisposition to such disorders

* The effect is strongly associated with initial marijuana use early in adolescence.

to the fact that the brain, including the endocannabinoid system, undergoes active development during adolescence.[6] Indeed, early and regular marijuana use predicts an increased risk of marijuana addiction, which in turn predicts an increased risk of the use of other illicit drugs.[7] As compared with persons who begin to use marijuana in adulthood, those who begin in adolescence are approximately 2 to 4 times as likely to have symptoms of cannabis dependence within 2 years after first use.[8]

EFFECT ON BRAIN DEVELOPMENT

The brain remains in a state of active, experience-guided development from the prenatal period through childhood and adolescence until the age of approximately 21 years.[9] During these developmental periods, it is intrinsically more vulnerable than a mature brain to the adverse long-term effects of environmental insults, such as exposure to tetrahydrocannabinol, or THC, the primary active ingredient in marijuana. This view has received considerable support from studies in animals, which have shown, for example, that prenatal or adolescent exposure to

THC can recalibrate the sensitivity of the reward system to other drugs[10] and that prenatal exposure interferes with cytoskeletal dynamics, which are critical for the establishment of axonal connections between neurons.[11]

As compared with unexposed controls, adults who smoked marijuana regularly during adolescence have impaired neural connectivity (fewer fibers) in specific brain regions. These include the precuneus, a key node that is involved in functions that require a high degree of integration (e.g., alertness and self-conscious awareness), and the fimbria, an area of the hippocampus that is important in learning and memory.[12] Reduced functional connectivity has also been reported in the prefrontal networks responsible for executive function (including inhibitory control) and the subcortical networks, which process habits and routines.[13] In addition, imaging studies in persons who use cannabis have revealed decreased activity in prefrontal regions and reduced volumes in the hippocampus.[14] Thus, certain brain regions may be more vulnerable than others to the long-term effects of marijuana. One study showed that selective down-regulation of cannabinoid-1 (CB1) receptors in several cortical brain regions in long-term marijuana smokers was correlated with years of cannabis smoking and was reversible after 4 weeks of abstinence.[15] Changes in CB1 receptors were not seen in subcortical regions.

The negative effect of marijuana use on the functional connectivity of the brain is particularly prominent if use starts in adolescence or young adulthood,[12] which may help to explain the finding of an association between frequent use of marijuana from adolescence into adulthood and significant declines in IQ.[16] The impairments in brain connectivity associated with exposure to marijuana in adolescence are consistent with preclinical findings indicating that the cannabinoid system plays a prominent role in synapse formation during brain development.[17]

POSSIBLE ROLE AS GATEWAY DRUG

Epidemiologic and preclinical data suggest that the use of marijuana in adolescence could influence multiple addictive behaviors in adulthood. In rodents exposed to cannabinoids during adolescence, there is decreased reactivity of the dopamine neurons that modulate the brain's reward regions.[18] The exposure of rodents to cannabis in utero alters the developmental regulation of the mesolimbic dopamine system of affected offspring.[19] If reduced dopamine reactivity in the brain's reward regions does follow early exposure to marijuana, this effect could help to explain the increased susceptibility to drug abuse and addiction to several drugs later in life, which has been reported in most epidemiologic studies.[20] This theory is also consistent with animal models showing that THC can prime the brain for enhanced responses to other drugs.[21] Although these findings support the idea that marijuana is a gateway drug, other drugs, such as alcohol and nicotine, can also be categorized as gateway drugs, since they also prime the brain for a heightened response to other drugs.[22] However, an alternative explanation is that people who are more susceptible to drug-taking behavior are simply more likely to start with marijuana because of its accessibility and that their subsequent social interactions with other drug users would increase the probability that they would try other drugs.

RELATION TO MENTAL ILLNESS

Regular marijuana use is associated with an increased risk of anxiety and depression,[23] but causality has not been established. Marijuana is also linked with psychoses (including those associated with schizophrenia), especially among people with a preexisting genetic vulnerability,[24] and exacerbates the course of illness in patients with schizophrenia. Heavier marijuana use, greater drug potency, and exposure at a younger age can all negatively affect the disease trajectory (e.g., by advancing the time of a first psychotic episode by 2 to 6 years).[25]

However, it is inherently difficult to establish causality in these types of studies because factors other than marijuana use may be directly associated with the risk of mental illness. In addition, other factors could predispose a person to both marijuana use and mental illness. This makes it difficult to confidently attribute the increased risk of mental illness to marijuana use.

EFFECT ON SCHOOL PERFORMANCE AND LIFETIME ACHIEVEMENT

In the 2013 Monitoring the Future survey of high-school students,[26] 6.5% of students in grade 12 reported daily or near-daily marijuana use, and this figure probably represents an underesti-

mate of use, since young people who have dropped out of school may have particularly high rates of frequent marijuana use.[27] Since marijuana use impairs critical cognitive functions, both during acute intoxication and for days after use,[28] many students could be functioning at a cognitive level that is below their natural capability for considerable periods of time. Although acute effects may subside after THC is cleared from the brain, it nonetheless poses serious risks to health that can be expected to accumulate with long-term or heavy use. The evidence suggests that such use results in measurable and long-lasting cognitive impairments,[16] particularly among those who started to use marijuana in early adolescence. Moreover, failure to learn at school, even for short or sporadic periods (a secondary effect of acute intoxication), will interfere with the subsequent capacity to achieve increasingly challenging educational goals, a finding that may also explain the association between regular marijuana use and poor grades.[29]

The relationship between cannabis use by young people and psychosocial harm is likely to be multifaceted, which may explain the inconsistencies among studies. For example, some studies suggest that long-term deficits may be reversible and remain subtle rather than disabling once a person abstains from use.[30] Other studies show that long-term, heavy use of marijuana results in impairments in memory and attention that persist and worsen with increasing years of regular use[31] and with the initiation of use during adolescence.[32] As noted above, early marijuana use is associated with impaired school performance and an increased risk of dropping out of school,[27,29] although reports of shared environmental factors that influence the risks of using cannabis at a young age and dropping out of school[33] suggest that the relationship may be more complex. Heavy marijuana use has been linked to lower income, greater need for socioeconomic assistance, unemployment, criminal behavior, and lower satisfaction with life.[2,34]

RISK OF MOTOR-VEHICLE ACCIDENTS

Both immediate exposure and long-term exposure to marijuana impair driving ability; marijuana is the illicit drug most frequently reported in connection with impaired driving and accidents, including fatal accidents.[35] There is a relationship between the blood THC concentration and performance in controlled driving-simulation studies,[36] which are a good predictor of real-world driving ability. Recent marijuana smoking and blood THC levels of 2 to 5 ng per milliliter are associated with substantial driving impairment.[37] According to a meta-analysis, the overall risk of involvement in an accident increases by a factor of about 2 when a person drives soon after using marijuana.[37] In an accident culpability analysis, persons testing positive for THC (typical minimum level of detection, 1 ng per milliliter), and particularly those with higher blood levels, were 3 to 7 times as likely to be responsible for a motor-vehicle accident as persons who had not used drugs or alcohol before driving.[38] In comparison, the overall risk of a vehicular accident increases by a factor of almost 5 for drivers with a blood alcohol level above 0.08%, the legal limit in most countries, and increases by a factor of 27 for persons younger than 21 years of age.[39] Not surprisingly, the risk associated with the use of alcohol in combination with marijuana appears to be greater than that associated with the use of either drug alone.[37]

RISK OF CANCER AND OTHER EFFECTS ON HEALTH

The effects of long-term marijuana smoking on the risk of lung cancer are unclear. For example, the use of marijuana for the equivalent of 30 or more joint-years (with 1 joint-year of marijuana use equal to 1 cigarette [joint] of marijuana smoked per day for 1 year) was associated with an increased incidence of lung cancer and several cancers of the upper aerodigestive tract; however, the association disappeared after adjustment for potential confounders such as cigarette smoking.[40] Although the possibility of a positive association between marijuana smoking and cancer cannot be ruled out,[41] the evidence suggests that the risk is lower with marijuana than with tobacco.[40] However, the smoking of cigarettes that contain both marijuana and tobacco products is a potential confounding factor with a prevalence that varies dramatically among countries.

Marijuana smoking is also associated with inflammation of the large airways, increased airway resistance, and lung hyperinflation, associations that are consistent with the fact that regular marijuana smokers are more likely to report symptoms of chronic bronchitis than are nonsmokers[42]; however, the long-term effect of low levels of marijuana exposure does not ap-

pear to be significant.[43] The immunologic competence of the respiratory system in marijuana smokers may also be compromised, as indicated by increased rates of respiratory infections and pneumonia.[44] Marijuana use has also been associated with vascular conditions that increase the risks of myocardial infarction, stroke, and transient ischemic attacks during marijuana intoxication.[45] The actual mechanisms underlying the effects of marijuana on the cardiovascular and cerebrovascular systems are complex and not fully understood. However, the direct effects of cannabinoids on various target receptors (i.e., CB1 receptors in arterial blood vessels) and the indirect effects on vasoactive compounds[46] may help explain the detrimental effects of marijuana on vascular resistance and coronary microcirculation.[47]

LIMITATIONS OF THE EVIDENCE AND GAPS IN KNOWLEDGE

Most of the long-term effects of marijuana use that are summarized here have been observed among heavy or long-term users, but multiple (often hidden) confounding factors detract from our ability to establish causality (including the frequent use of marijuana in combination with other drugs). These factors also complicate our ability to assess the true effect of intrauterine exposure to marijuana. Indeed, despite the use of marijuana by pregnant women,[48] and animal models suggesting that cannabis exposure during pregnancy may alter the normal processes and trajectories of brain development,[49] our understanding of the long-term effects of prenatal exposure to marijuana in humans is very poor.

The THC content, or potency, of marijuana, as detected in confiscated samples, has been steadily increasing from about 3% in the 1980s to 12% in 2012[50] (Fig. 1A). This increase in THC content raises concerns that the consequences of marijuana use may be worse now than in the past and may account for the significant increases in emergency department visits by persons reporting marijuana use[51] (Fig. 1B) and the increases in fatal motor-vehicle accidents.[35] This increase in THC potency over time also raises questions about the current relevance of the findings in older studies on the effects of marijuana use, especially studies that assessed long-term outcomes.

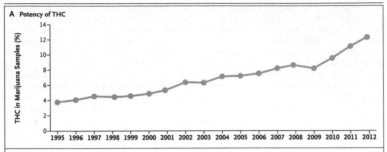

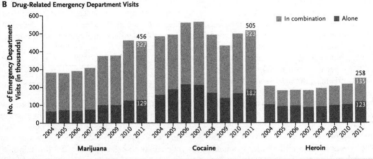

Figure 1. Increases over Time in the Potency of Tetrahydrocannabinol (THC) in Marijuana and the Number of Emergency Department Visits Involving Marijuana, Cocaine, or Heroin.

Panel A shows the increasing potency of marijuana (i.e., the percentage of THC) in samples seized by the Drug Enforcement Administration (DEA) between 1995 and 2012.[50] Panel B provides estimates of the number of emergency department visits involving the use of selected illicit drugs (marijuana, cocaine, and heroin) either singly or in combination with other drugs between 2004 and 2011.[51] Among these three drugs, only marijuana, used either in combination with other drugs or alone, was associated with significant increases in the number of visits during this period (a 62% increase when used in combination with other drugs and a 100% increase when used alone, P<0.05 for the two comparisons).

There is also a need to improve our understanding of how to harness the potential medical benefits of the marijuana plant without exposing people who are sick to its intrinsic risks. The authoritative report by the Institute of Medicine, *Marijuana and Medicine*,[52] acknowledges the potential benefits of smoking marijuana in stimulating appetite, particularly in patients with the acquired immunodeficiency syndrome (AIDS) and the related wasting syndrome, and in combating chemotherapy-induced nausea and vomiting, severe pain, and some forms of spasticity. The report also indicates that there is some evidence for the benefit of using marijuana to decrease intraocular pressure in the treatment of glaucoma. Nonetheless, the report stresses the importance of focusing research efforts on the therapeutic potential of synthetic or pharmaceutically pure cannabinoids.[52] Some physicians continue to prescribe marijuana for medicinal purposes despite limited evidence of a benefit (see box). This practice raises particular concerns with regard to long-term use by vulnerable populations. For example, there is some evidence to suggest that in patients with symptoms of human immunodeficiency virus (HIV) infection or AIDS, marijuana use may actually exacerbate HIV-associated cognitive deficits.[75] Simi-

---

Clinical Conditions with Symptoms That May Be Relieved by Treatment with Marijuana or Other Cannabinoids.*

Glaucoma

Early evidence of the benefits of marijuana in patients with glaucoma (a disease associated with increased pressure in the eye) may be consistent with its ability to effect a transient decrease in intraocular pressure,[53,54] but other, standard treatments are currently more effective. THC, cannabinol, and nabilone (a synthetic cannabinoid similar to THC), but not cannabidiol, were shown to lower intraocular pressure in rabbits.[55,56] More research is needed to establish whether molecules that modulate the endocannabinoid system may not only reduce intraocular pressure but also provide a neuroprotective benefit in patients with glaucoma.[57]

Nausea

Treatment of the nausea and vomiting associated with chemotherapy was one of the first medical uses of THC and other cannabinoids.[58] THC is an effective antiemetic agent in patients undergoing chemotherapy,[59] but patients often state that marijuana is more effective in suppressing nausea. Other, unidentified compounds in marijuana may enhance the effect of THC (as appears to be the case with THC and cannabidiol, which operate through different antiemetic mechanisms).[60] Paradoxically, increased vomiting (hyperemesis) has been reported with repeated marijuana use.

AIDS-associated anorexia and wasting syndrome

Reports have indicated that smoked or ingested cannabis improves appetite and leads to weight gain and improved mood and quality of life among patients with AIDS.[61] However, there is no long-term or rigorous evidence of a sustained effect of cannabis on AIDS-related morbidity and mortality, with an acceptable safety profile, that would justify its incorporation into current clinical practice for patients who are receiving effective antiretroviral therapy.[62] Data from the few studies that have explored the potential therapeutic value of cannabinoids for this patient population are inconclusive.[62]

Chronic pain

Marijuana has been used to relieve pain for centuries. Studies have shown that cannabinoids acting through central CB1 receptors, and possibly peripheral CB1 and CB2 receptors,[63] play important roles in modeling nociceptive responses in various models of pain. These findings are consistent with reports that marijuana may be effective in ameliorating neuropathic pain,[64,65] even at very low levels of THC (1.29%).[66] Both marijuana and dronabinol, a pharmaceutical formulation of THC, decrease pain, but dronabinol may lead to longer-lasting reductions in pain sensitivity and lower ratings of rewarding effects.[67]

Inflammation

Cannabinoids (e.g., THC and cannabidiol) have substantial antiinflammatory effects because of their ability to induce apoptosis, inhibit cell proliferation, and suppress cytokine production.[68] Cannabidiol has attracted particular interest as an antiinflammatory agent because of its lack of psychoactive effects.[58] Animal models have shown that cannabidiol is a promising candidate for the treatment of rheumatoid arthritis[58] and for inflammatory diseases of the gastrointestinal tract (e.g., ulcerative colitis and Crohn's disease).[69]

Multiple sclerosis

Nabiximols (Sativex, GW Pharmaceuticals), an oromucosal spray that delivers a mix of THC and cannabidiol, appears to be an effective treatment for neuropathic pain, disturbed sleep, and spasticity in patients with multiple sclerosis. Sativex is available in the United Kingdom, Canada, and several other countries[70,71] and is currently being reviewed in phase 3 trials in the United States in order to gain approval from the Food and Drug Administration.

Epilepsy

In a recent small survey of parents who use marijuana with a high cannabidiol content to treat epileptic seizures in their children,[72] 11% (2 families out of the 19 that met the inclusion criteria) reported complete freedom from seizures, 42% (8 families) reported a reduction of more than 80% in seizure frequency, and 32% (6 families) reported a reduction of 25 to 60% in seizure frequency. Although such reports are promising, insufficient safety and efficacy data are available on the use of cannabis botanicals for the treatment of epilepsy.[73] However, there is increasing evidence of the role of cannabidiol as an antiepileptic agent in animal models.[74]

---

* AIDS denotes acquired immunodeficiency syndrome, CB1 cannabinoid-1 receptor, and CB2 cannabinoid-2 receptor, HIV human immunodeficiency virus, and THC tetrahydrocannabinol.

---

larly, more research is needed to understand the potential effects of marijuana use on age-related cognitive decline in general and on memory impairment in particular.

Research is needed on the ways in which government policies on marijuana affect public health outcomes. Our understanding of the effects of policy on market forces is quite limited (e.g., the allure of new tax-revenue streams from the legal sale of marijuana, pricing wars, youth-targeted advertising, and the emergence of cannabis-based medicines approved by the Food and Drug Administration), as is our understanding of the interrelated variables of perceptions about

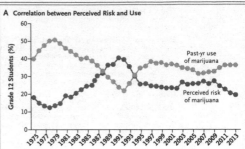

Figure 2. Use of Marijuana in Relation to Perceived Risk and Daily Use of Tobacco Cigarettes or Marijuana among U.S. Students in Grade 12, 1975–2013.

Panel A shows the inverse correlation between the perception of the risk associated with marijuana use and actual use. Perceived risk corresponds to the percentage of teenagers who reported that the use of marijuana is dangerous. Panel B shows the percentage of students who reported daily use of tobacco cigarettes or marijuana in the previous 30 days. Data for both graphs are from Johnston et al.[26]

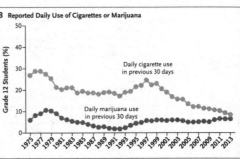

use, types of use, and outcomes. Historically, there has been an inverse correlation between marijuana use and the perception of its risks among adolescents (Fig. 2A). Assuming that this inverse relationship is causal, would greater permissiveness in culture and social policy lead to an increase in the number of young people who are exposed to cannabis on a regular basis? Among students in grade 12, the reported prevalence of regular marijuana smoking has been steadily increasing in recent years and may soon intersect the trend line for regular tobacco smoking (Fig. 2B). We also need information about the effects of second-hand exposure to cannabis smoke and cannabinoids. Second-hand exposure is an important public health issue in the context of tobacco smoking, but we do not have a clear understanding of the effects of second-hand exposure to marijuana smoking.[76] Studies in states (e.g., Colorado, California, and Washington) and countries (e.g., Uruguay, Portugal, and the Netherlands) where social and legal policies are shifting may provide important data for shaping future policies.

CONCLUSIONS

Marijuana use has been associated with substantial adverse effects, some of which have been determined with a high level of confidence (Table 2). Marijuana, like other drugs of abuse, can result in addiction. During intoxication, marijuana can interfere with cognitive function (e.g., memory and perception of time) and motor function (e.g., coordination), and these effects can have detrimental consequences (e.g., motor-vehicle accidents). Repeated marijuana use during adolescence may result in long-lasting changes in brain function that can jeopardize educational, professional, and social achievements. However, the ef-

Table 2. Level of Confidence in the Evidence for Adverse Effects of Marijuana on Health and Well-Being.

Effect	Overall Level of Confidence*
Addiction to marijuana and other substances	High
Abnormal brain development	Medium
Progression to use of other drugs	Medium
Schizophrenia	Medium
Depression or anxiety	Medium
Diminished lifetime achievement	High
Motor vehicle accidents	High
Symptoms of chronic bronchitis	High
Lung cancer	Low

* The indicated overall level of confidence in the association between marijuana use and the listed effects represents an attempt to rank the strength of the current evidence, especially with regard to heavy or long-term use and use that starts in adolescence.

fects of a drug (legal or illegal) on individual health are determined not only by its pharmacologic properties but also by its availability and social acceptability. In this respect, legal drugs (alcohol and tobacco) offer a sobering perspective, accounting for the greatest burden of disease associated with drugs[77] not because they are more dangerous than illegal drugs but because their legal status allows for more widespread exposure. As policy shifts toward legalization of marijuana, it is reasonable and probably prudent to hypothesize that its use will increase and that, by extension, so will the number of persons for whom there will be negative health consequences.

No potential conflict of interest relevant to this article was reported.

Disclosure forms provided by the authors are available with the full text of this article at NEJM.org.

REFERENCES

1. Center for Behavioral Health Statistics and Quality. National survey on drug use and health. Rockville, MD: Substance Abuse & Mental Health Services Administration, 2013.
2. Fergusson DM, Boden JM. Cannabis use and later life outcomes. Addiction 2008;103:969-76.
3. Lopez-Quintero C, Pérez de los Cobos J, Hasin DS, et al. Probability and predictors of transition from first use to dependence on nicotine, alcohol, cannabis, and cocaine: results of the National Epidemiologic Survey on Alcohol and Related Conditions (NESARC). Drug Alcohol Depend 2011;115:120-30.
4. Hall W, Degenhardt L. Adverse health effects of non-medical cannabis use. Lancet 2009;374:1383-91.
5. Gorelick DA, Levin KH, Copersino ML, et al. Diagnostic criteria for cannabis withdrawal syndrome. Drug Alcohol Depend 2012;123:141-7.
6. Mechoulam R, Parker LA. The endocannabinoid system and the brain. Annu Rev Psychol 2013;64:21-47.
7. Hall W, Degenhardt L. Prevalence and correlates of cannabis use in developed and developing countries. Curr Opin Psychiatry 2007;20:393-7.
8. Chen CY, Storr CL, Anthony JC. Early-onset drug use and risk for drug dependence problems. Addict Behav 2009;34: 319-22.
9. Gogtay N, Giedd JN, Lusk L, et al. Dynamic mapping of human cortical development during childhood through early adulthood. Proc Natl Acad Sci U S A 2004;101:8174-9.
10. Dinieri JA, Hurd YL. Rat models of prenatal and adolescent cannabis exposure. Methods Mol Biol 2012;829:231-42.
11. Tortoriello G, Morris CV, Alpar A, et al. Miswiring the brain: Δ9-tetrahydrocannabinol disrupts cortical development by inducing an SCG10/stathmin-2 degradation pathway. EMBO J 2014;33:668-85.
12. Zalesky A, Solowij N, Yücel M, et al. Effect of long-term cannabis use on axonal fibre connectivity. Brain 2012;135: 2245-55.
13. Filbey F, Yezhuvath U. Functional connectivity in inhibitory control networks and severity of cannabis use disorder. Am J Drug Alcohol Abuse 2013;39:382-91.
14. Batalla A, Bhattacharyya S, Yücel M,

et al. Structural and functional imaging studies in chronic cannabis users: a systematic review of adolescent and adult findings. PLoS One 2013;8(2):e55821.
15. Hirvonen J, Goodwin RS, Li C-T, et al. Reversible and regionally selective downregulation of brain cannabinoid CB1 receptors in chronic daily cannabis smokers. Mol Psychiatry 2012;17:642-9.
16. Meier MH, Caspi A, Ambler A, et al. Persistent cannabis users show neuropsychological decline from childhood to midlife. Proc Natl Acad Sci U S A 2012;109(40): E2657-E2564.
17. Gaffuri AL, Ladarre D, Lenkei Z. Type-1 cannabinoid receptor signaling in neuronal development. Pharmacology 2012;90:19-39.
18. Pistis M, Perra S, Pillolla G, Melis M, Muntoni AL, Gessa GL. Adolescent exposure to cannabinoids induces long-lasting changes in the response to drugs of abuse of rat midbrain dopamine neurons. Biol Psychiatry 2004;56:86-94.
19. DiNieri JA, Wang X, Szutorisz H, et al. Maternal cannabis use alters ventral striatal dopamine D2 gene regulation in the offspring. Biol Psychiatry 2011;70:763-9.
20. Agrawal A, Neale MC, Prescott CA, Kendler KS. A twin study of early cannabis use and subsequent use and abuse/ dependence of other illicit drugs. Psychol Med 2004;34:1227-37.
21. Panlilio LV, Zanettini C, Barnes C, Solinas M, Goldberg SR. Prior exposure to THC increases the addictive effects of nicotine in rats. Neuropsychopharmacology 2013;38:1198-208.
22. Levine A, Huang Y, Drisaldi B, et al. Molecular mechanism for a gateway drug: epigenetic changes initiated by nicotine prime gene expression by cocaine. Sci Transl Med 2011;3:107ra109.
23. Patton GC, Coffey C, Carlin JB, Degenhardt L, Lynskey M, Hall W. Cannabis use and mental health in young people: cohort study. BMJ 2002;325:1195-8.
24. Caspi A, Moffitt TE, Cannon M, et al. Moderation of the effect of adolescent-onset cannabis use on adult psychosis by a functional polymorphism in the catechol-O-methyltransferase gene: longitudinal evidence of a gene X environment interaction. Biol Psychiatry 2005;57:1117-27.
25. Di Forti M, Sallis H, Allegri F, et al. Daily use, especially of high-potency can-

nabis, drives the earlier onset of psychosis in cannabis users. Schizophr Bull 2014 March 19 (Epub ahead of print).
26. Johnston LD, O'Malley PM, Miech RA, et al. Monitoring the Future: national survey results on drug use, 1975-2013 — overview, key findings on adolescent drug use. Ann Arbor: Institute for Social Research, University of Michigan, 2014 (http://monitoringthefuture.org/pubs/monographs/mtf-overview2013.pdf).
27. Bray JW, Zarkin GA, Ringwalt C, Qi J. The relationship between marijuana initiation and dropping out of high school. Health Econ 2000;9:9-18.
28. Crean RD, Crane NA, Mason BJ. An evidence based review of acute and long-term effects of cannabis use on executive cognitive functions. J Addict Med 2011; 5:1-8.
29. Lynskey M, Hall W. The effects of adolescent cannabis use on educational attainment: a review. Addiction 2000;95: 1621-30.
30. Macleod J, Oakes R, Copello A, et al. Psychological and social sequelae of cannabis and other illicit drug use by young people: a systematic review of longitudinal, general population studies. Lancet 2004;363:1579-88.
31. Solowij N, Stephens RS, Roffman RA, et al. Cognitive functioning of long-term heavy cannabis users seeking treatment. JAMA 2002;287:1123-31. [Erratum, JAMA 2002;287:1651.]
32. Schweinsburg AD, Brown SA, Tapert SF. The influence of marijuana use on neurocognitive functioning in adolescents. Curr Drug Abuse Rev 2008;1:99-111.
33. Verweij KJ, Huizink AC, Agrawal A, Martin NG, Lynskey MT. Is the relationship between early-onset cannabis use and educational attainment causal or due to common liability? Drug Alcohol Depend 2013;133:580-6.
34. Brook JS, Lee JY, Finch SJ, Seltzer N, Brook DW. Adult work commitment, financial stability, and social environment as related to trajectories of marijuana use beginning in adolescence. Subst Abus 2013;34:298-305.
35. Brady JE, Li G. Trends in alcohol and other drugs detected in fatally injured drivers in the United States, 1999-2010. Am J Epidemiol 2014;179:692-9.
36. Lenné MG, Dietze PM, Triggs TJ,

Walmsley S, Murphy B, Redman JR. The effects of cannabis and alcohol on simulated arterial driving: influences of driving experience and task demand. Accid Anal Prev 2010;42:859-66.

37. Hartman RL, Huestis MA. Cannabis effects on driving skills. Clin Chem 2013; 59:478-92.

38. Ramaekers JG, Berghaus G, van Laar M, Drummer OH. Dose related risk of motor vehicle crashes after cannabis use. Drug Alcohol Depend 2004;73:109-19.

39. Peck RC, Gebers MA, Voas RB, Romano E. The relationship between blood alcohol concentration (BAC), age, and crash risk. J Safety Res 2008;39:311-9.

40. Hashibe M, Morgenstern H, Cui Y, et al. Marijuana use and the risk of lung and upper aerodigestive tract cancers: results of a population-based case-control study. Cancer Epidemiol Biomarkers Prev 2006; 15:1829-34.

41. Callaghan RC, Allebeck P, Sidorchuk A. Marijuana use and risk of lung cancer: a 40-year cohort study. Cancer Causes Control 2013;24:1811-20.

42. Tashkin DP. Effects of marijuana smoking on the lung. Ann Am Thorac Soc 2013;10:239-47.

43. Pletcher MJ, Vittinghoff E, Kalhan R, et al. Association between marijuana exposure and pulmonary function over 20 years. JAMA 2012;307:173-81.

44. Owen KP, Sutter ME, Albertson TE. Marijuana: respiratory tract effects. Clin Rev Allergy Immunol 2014;46:65-81.

45. Thomas G, Kloner RA, Rezkalla S. Adverse cardiovascular, cerebrovascular, and peripheral vascular effects of marijuana inhalation: what cardiologists need to know. Am J Cardiol 2014;113:187-90.

46. Stanley C, O'Sullivan SE. Vascular targets for cannabinoids: animal and human studies. Br J Pharmacol 2014;171:1361-78.

47. Rezkalla SH, Sharma P, Kloner RA. Coronary no-flow and ventricular tachycardia associated with habitual marijuana use. Ann Emerg Med 2003;42:365-9.

48. Brown HL, Graves CR. Smoking and marijuana use in pregnancy. Clin Obstet Gynecol 2013;56:107-13.

49. Jutras-Aswad D, DiNieri JA, Harkany T, Hurd YL. Neurobiological consequences of maternal cannabis on human fetal development and its neuropsychiatric outcome. Eur Arch Psychiatry Clin Neurosci 2009;259:395-412.

50. ElSohly MA. Potency Monitoring Program quarterly report no.123 — reporting period: 09/16/2013-12/15/2013. Oxford:

University of Mississippi, National Center for Natural Products Research, 2014.

51. Drug Abuse Warning Network, 2011: national estimates of drug-related emergency department visits. Rockville, MD: Substance Abuse and Mental Health Services Administration, 2011 (http://www .samhsa.gov/data/2k13/DAWN2k11ED/ DAWN2k11ED.htm).

52. Joy JE, Watson SJ Jr, Benson JA Jr, eds. Marijuana and medicine: assessing the science base. Washington, DC: National Academy Press, 1999.

53. Merritt JC, Crawford WJ, Alexander PC, Anduze AL, Gelbart SS. Effect of marihuana on intraocular and blood pressure in glaucoma. Ophthalmology 1980;87:222-8.

54. Hepler RS, Frank IR. Marihuana smoking and intraocular pressure. JAMA 1971;217:1392.

55. Chen J, Matias I, Dinh T, et al. Finding of endocannabinoids in human eye tissues: implications for glaucoma. Biochem Biophys Res Commun 2005;330:1062-7.

56. Song ZH, Slowey CA. Involvement of cannabinoid receptors in the intraocular pressure-lowering effects of WIN55212-2. J Pharmacol Exp Ther 2000;292:136-9.

57. Nucci C, Bari M, Spanò A, et al. Potential roles of (endo) cannabinoids in the treatment of glaucoma: from intraocular pressure control to neuroprotection. Prog Brain Res 2008;173:451-64.

58. Zuardi AW. Cannabidiol: from an inactive cannabinoid to a drug with wide spectrum of action. Rev Bras Psiquiatr 2008;30:271-80.

59. Sallan SE, Zinberg NE, Frei E III. Antiemetic effect of delta-9-tetrahydrocannabinol in patients receiving cancer chemotherapy. N Engl J Med 1975;293:795-7.

60. Parker LA, Kwiatkowska M, Burton P, Mechoulam R. Effect of cannabinoids on lithium-induced vomiting in the Suncus murinus (house musk shrew). Psychopharmacology (Berl) 2004;171:156-61.

61. D'Souza G, Matson PA, Grady CD, et al. Medicinal and recreational marijuana use among HIV-infected women in the Women's Interagency HIV Study (WIHS) cohort, 1994-2010. J Acquir Immune Defic Syndr 2012;61:618-26.

62. Lutge EE, Gray A, Siegfried N. The medical use of cannabis for reducing morbidity and mortality in patients with HIV/AIDS. Cochrane Database Syst Rev 2013;4:CD005175.

63. Chiou LC, Hu SS, Ho YC. Targeting the cannabinoid system for pain relief? Acta Anaesthesiol Taiwan 2013;51:161-70.

64. Wilsey B, Marcotte T, Tsodikov A, et al. A randomized, placebo-controlled, crossover trial of cannabis cigarettes in neuropathic pain. J Pain 2008;9:506-21.

65. Wallace M, Schulteis G, Atkinson JH, et al. Dose-dependent effects of smoked cannabis on capsaicin-induced pain and hyperalgesia in healthy volunteers. Anesthesiology 2007;107:785-96.

66. Wilsey B, Marcotte T, Deutsch R, Gouaux B, Sakai S, Donaghe H. Low-dose vaporized cannabis significantly improves neuropathic pain. J Pain 2013;14:136-48.

67. Cooper ZD, Comer SD, Haney M. Comparison of the analgesic effects of dronabinol and smoked marijuana in daily marijuana smokers. Neuropsychopharmacology 2013;38:1984-92.

68. Nagarkatti P, Pandey R, Rieder SA, Hegde VL, Nagarkatti M. Cannabinoids as novel anti-inflammatory drugs. Future Med Chem 2009;1:1333-49.

69. Esposito G, Filippis DD, Cirillo C, et al. Cannabidiol in inflammatory bowel diseases: a brief overview. Phytother Res 2013;5:633-6.

70. Collin C, Davies P, Mutiboko IK, Ratcliffe S. Randomized controlled trial of cannabis-based medicine in spasticity caused by multiple sclerosis. Eur J 2007; 14:290-6.

71. Centonze D, Mori F, Koch G, et al. Lack of effect of cannabis-based treatment on clinical and laboratory measures in multiple sclerosis. Neurol Sci 2009;30:531-4.

72. Porter BE, Jacobson C. Report of a parent survey of cannabidiol-enriched cannabis use in pediatric treatment-resistant epilepsy. Epilepsy Behav 2013;29:574-7.

73. Kogan NM, Mechoulam R. Cannabinoids in health and disease. Dialogues Clin Neurosci 2007;9:413-30.

74. Hill TD, Cascio MG, Romano B, et al. Cannabidivarin-rich cannabis extracts are anticonvulsant in mouse and rat via a CB1 receptor-independent mechanism. Br J Pharmacol 2013;170:679-92.

75. Cristiani SA, Pukay-Martin ND, Bornstein RA. Marijuana use and cognitive function in HIV-infected people. J Neuropsychiatry Clin Neurosci 2004;16:330-5.

76. Niedbala S, Kardos K, Salamone S, Fritch D, Bronsgeest M, Cone EJ. Passive cannabis smoke exposure and oral fluid testing. J Anal Toxicol 2004;28:546-52.

77. Degenhardt L, Hall W. Extent of illicit drug use and dependence, and their contribution to the global burden of disease. Lancet 2012;379:55-70.

Copyright © 2014 Massachusetts Medical Society.

IMAGES IN CLINICAL MEDICINE

The *Journal* welcomes consideration of new submissions for Images in Clinical Medicine. Instructions for authors and procedures for submissions can be found on the *Journal's* website at NEJM.org. At the discretion of the editor, images that are accepted for publication may appear in the print version of the *Journal*, the electronic version, or both.

Adverse Health Effects of Marijuana Use

TO THE EDITOR: In their article, Volkow et al. (June 5 issue)[1] state that marijuana may have adverse health effects, particularly on the vulnerable brains of young people. Potential mechanisms underlying the effect of marijuana on the cerebrovascular system are indeed complex, although a temporal relationship between the use of marijuana (natural or synthetic) and stroke in young people has recently been described.[2,3] Simultaneously, the presence of multifocal intracranial arterial vasoconstriction was observed, which was reversible in some cases after cessation of cannabis exposure.[3] Thus, stroke, which is still underdiagnosed, may potentially play a role in neuronal damage related to marijuana use, even in young people without cardiovascular risk factors. Furthermore, tetrahydrocannabinol (THC), a major component of cannabis, has been shown experimentally to impair the function of the mitochondrial respiratory chain and to increase the production of reactive oxygen species in the brain.[4] Both of these processes are key events during stroke,[5] suggesting that THC may also increase a patient's vulnerability to stroke. In the ongoing shift toward marijuana legalization, physicians should probably inform marijuana users, whether they are using it for recreational purposes or therapeutic indications, about the risk of stroke with potential severe disability.

Valérie Wolff, M.D.
Olivier Rouyer, M.D., Ph.D.
Bernard Geny, M.D., Ph.D.
Fédération de Médecine Translationnelle
  de Strasbourg
Strasbourg, France
bernard.geny@chru-strasbourg.fr

No potential conflict of interest relevant to this letter was reported.

1. Volkow ND, Baler RD, Compton WM, Weiss SRB. Adverse health effects of marijuana use. N Engl J Med 2014;370:2219-27.
2. Freeman MJ, Rose DZ, Myers MA, Gooch CL, Bozeman AC, Burgin WS. Ischemic stroke after use of the synthetic marijuana "spice." Neurology 2013;81:2090-3.
3. Wolff V, Armspach JP, Lauer V, et al. Cannabis-related stroke: myth or reality? Stroke 2013;44:558-63.
4. Wolff V, Rouyer O, Schlagowski A, et al. Etude de l'effet du THC sur la respiration mitochondriale du cerveau de rat: une piste de réflexion pour expliquer le lien entre la consommation de cannabis et la survenue d'infarctus cérébral chez l'homme. Rev Neurol 2014 (http://dx.doi.ORG/10.1016/j.neurol.2014.01.081).
5. Sims NR, Muyderman H. Mitochondria, oxidative metabolism and cell death in stroke. Biochim Biophys Acta 2010;1802:80-91.

DOI: 10.1056/NEJMc1407928

TO THE EDITOR: Volkow et al. focus primarily on the neurocognitive and societal effects of marijuana use. We wish to note the known and potentially unknown infectious risks of marijuana, which were not discussed.

Recreational use of marijuana has been associated with a multistate outbreak of salmonellosis, illustrating the potential for widespread exposure through either inadvertent contamination during growing and storage or purposeful adulteration.[1] More worrisome are the risks of marijuana use for medical purposes, particularly by the population of immunocompromised patients. Prior reports have documented the frequent contamination of marijuana with fungal organisms and the potential for severe complications, including death.[2-4] These risks are not well studied and thus are poorly defined.

To date, 23 states allow the medical use of marijuana; however, dispensaries are currently not subject to regulation or quality control. We believe that the infectious risks need to be better defined, which would allow for appropriate regulatory oversight. The current approach places patients (unknowingly) at undue risk for acquisition of severe, and often lethal, infections.

George R. Thompson III, M.D.
Joseph M. Tuscano, M.D.
University of California, Davis, Medical Center
Sacramento, CA
grthompson@ucdavis.edu

No potential conflict of interest relevant to this letter was reported.

1. Taylor DN, Wachsmuth IK, Shangkuan Y, et al. Salmonellosis associated with marijuana: a multistate outbreak traced by plasmid fingerprinting. N Engl J Med 1982;306:1249-53.
2. Kagen SL. Aspergillus: an inhalable contaminant of marihuana. N Engl J Med 1981;304:483-4.
3. Verwelj PE, Kerremans JJ, Voss A, Meis JF. Fungal contamination of tobacco and marijuana. JAMA 2000;284:2875.
4. Sipsas NV, Kontoyiannis DP. Occupation, lifestyle, diet, and invasive fungal infections. Infection 2008;36:515-25.

DOI: 10.1056/NEJMc1407928

TO THE EDITOR: One safety aspect that is not discussed by Volkow et al. is the potential for interactions between marijuana and medications. *Cannabis sativa Linnaeus* products contain more than 700 distinct chemical entities. The relative abundance of these chemical entities in marijuana products and in human plasma can vary considerably depending on numerous factors, including the geographic location of cultivation, the method of preparation or administration, and the cultivar administered.

In vitro studies have shown that constituents of cannabis are potent and broad-spectrum inhibitors of key drug-metabolizing enzymes and transporters, including CYP2C9, CYP2C19, CYP2D6, CYP2E1, CYP3A4, and P-glycoprotein.[1-4] Other data from in vitro studies suggest the potential for enzyme induction, especially of CYP1A2.

Case reports support the risk of pharmacokinetic interactions; however, clinical studies have been equivocal. Notably, these studies have not replicated the long-term high potency and high dose achieved by some marijuana users (e.g., hashish users). Health care providers need to maintain a high level of suspicion for drug interactions in their patients who use marijuana products.

Carol Collins, M.D.
University of Washington
Seattle, WA
carolc3@u.washington.edu

No potential conflict of interest relevant to this letter was reported.

1. Yamaori S, Koeda K, Kushihara M, Hada Y, Yamamoto I, Watanabe K. Comparison in the in vitro inhibitory effects of major phytocannabinoids and polycyclic aromatic hydrocarbons contained in marijuana smoke on cytochrome P450 2C9 activity. Drug Metab Pharmacokinet 2012;27:294-300.
2. Yamaori S, Okamoto Y, Yamamoto I, Watanabe K. Cannabidiol, a major phytocannabinoid, as a potent atypical inhibitor for CYP2D6. Drug Metab Dispos 2011;39:2049-56.
3. Yamaori S, Ebisawa J, Okushima Y, Yamamoto I, Watanabe K. Potent inhibition of human cytochrome P450 3A isoforms by cannabidiol: role of phenolic hydroxyl groups in the resorcinol moiety. Life Sci 2011;88:730-6.
4. Zhu H-JZ, Wang J-S, Markowitz JS, et al. Characterization of P-glycoprotein inhibition by major cannabinoids from marijuana. J Pharmacol Exp Ther 2006;317:850-7.

DOI: 10.1056/NEJMc1407928

THE AUTHORS REPLY: We thank Wolff et al., Thompson and Tuscano, and Collins for their correspondence regarding potential adverse consequences of marijuana use that were not explicitly highlighted in our recent review. Given the shifting landscape of marijuana use, it is critically important that we be on the lookout for the emergence of predictable or unexpected health effects. This is particularly important when it comes to the potential of marijuana to negatively affect persons with various medical conditions, to interact with specific medications, or to influence the course of heretofore unstudied conditions. It will also be important to support the targeted research needed to understand the effects, both positive and negative, that may result from patients experimenting with marijuana in an attempt to relieve their specific symptoms. These studies should also focus on the possibility that such patients may forego evidence-based treatments while chasing after the purported therapeutic benefits of marijuana. Finally, we encourage particular attention to research targeting the effects of marijuana and other substances on adolescents, whose actively developing brains make them a particularly vulnerable population.[1,2]

Nora D. Volkow, M.D.
Wilson M. Compton, M.D.
Susan R.B. Weiss, Ph.D.
National Institutes of Health
Bethesda, MD
nvolkow@nida.nih.gov

Since publication of their article, the authors report no further potential conflict of interest.

1. DuPont RL, Lieberman JA. Young brains on drugs. Science 2014;344:557.
2. Volkow ND, Koob G, Guttmacher A, Croyle R. National longitudinal study of the neurodevelopmental consequences of substance use. Bethesda, MD: National Institute on Drug Abuse, May 16, 2014 (http://www.drugabuse.gov/about-nida/noras-blog/2014/05/national-longitudinal-study-neurodevelopmental-consequences-substance-use).

DOI: 10.1056/NEJMc1407928

Notes

Introduction

1. "For First Time, Americans Favor Legalizing Marijuana": http://www.gallup.com/poll/165539/first-time-americans-favor-legalizing-marijuana.aspx
2. While many think marijuana is legal in the Netherlands, it actually is not. And it is of interest to us that even in the Netherlands, a pioneer in liberalized marijuana laws, efforts are now under way to crack down on use, especially near schools and by "drug tourists," those who go to the Netherlands because of its marijuana laws. As one recent CBS report put it: "The Netherlands, the world pioneer in pot liberalization, has recently taken a harder line toward marijuana." See http://www.cbsnews.com/news/while-us-states-relax-marijuana-laws-pot-haven-netherlands-cracks-down-with-mixed-success/
3. "Marijuana in California: Jerry Brown Opposes Legalization, Says 'We Need to Stay Alert' ": http://www.mercurynews.com/california/ci_25259988/california-governor-jerry-brown-opposes-legalizing-pot-because

Chapter 1: Marijuana Use Is Not Safe or Harmless. On the Contrary, It Is Dangerous.

1. "Going the Distance: On and off the Road with Barack Obama": http://www.newyorker.com/reporting/2014/01/27/140127fa_fact_remnick?currentPage=all
2. Ibid.
3. "Address to the Nation on the National Drug Control Strategy": http://www.presidency.ucsb.edu/ws/?pid=17472
4. Google search results: https://www.google.com/search?q=marijuana+teen+brain&ie=utf-8&oe=utf-8&aq=t&rls=org.mozilla:en-US:official&client=firefox-a&channel=fflb (visited March 5, 2014).
5. Google search results: https://www.google.com/search?num=100&client=firefox-a&hs=prs&rls=org.mozilla%3Aen-US%3Aofficial&channel=fflb&q=marijuana+psychosis&oq=marijuana+psychosis&gs_l=serp.3..019.10040077.10046800.0.10047070.25.17.3.5.5.0.161.1640.12j5.17.0....0...1c.1.37.serp..2.23.1384.OUU5mRIngNA (visited March 4, 2014).

6. "Longtime Marijuana Use Linked With Decreased Motivation, Study Finds": http://www.huffingtonpost.com/2013/07/02/marijuana-motivation-longtime -use-pot_n_3534031.html

7. Robert L. DuPont, MD. *The Selfish Brain* (Center City, MN: Hazelden, 1997), 146–147.

8. "Fast Facts": http://www.cdc.gov/tobacco/data-statistics/fact-sheets/fast-facts/

9. Alexandra Sifferlin, "Up in Smoke," *Time*, August 27, 2012.

10. "Arizona's Smoking Rate Drops 21 Percent; Ad Campaign, Higher Taxes Credited": http://community.seattletimes.nwsource.com/archive/?date=20010 525&slug=azsmoke25

11. Ibid.

12. "More Teens Smoke Pot Than Cigarettes, says CDC Survey": http://www .cbsnews.com/news/more-teens-smoke-pot-than-cigarettes-says-cdc-survey/

13. "Marijuana Policy Winds Shifting in California": http://www.californiahealth line.org/insight/2014/marijuana-policy-winds-shifting-in-calif

14. "I'm a Parent Who Smokes Pot": http://www.redbookmag.com/kids-family/ advice/pot-parents

15. Ibid.

16. Ibid.

17. "Better for Kids?": http://www.thestranger.com/slog/archives/2009/08/10/better -for-kids

18. "As Marijuana Laws Change, More Teens Think Drugs Are Safe": http://www .deseretnews.com/article/865596001/As-marijuana-laws-change-more-teens -think-drugs-are-safe.html?pg=all

19. Ibid.

20. "DrugFacts: Marijuana": http://www.drugabuse.gov/publications/drugfacts/ marijuana

21. "Marijuana": http://www.lung.org/associations/states/colorado/tobacco/mari juana.html

22. "Marijuana Smoking and the Risk of Lung Cancer: Time for Pause": http://www .swedish.org/about/blog/february-2013/marijuana-smoking-and-the-risk-of -lung-cancer

23. Ibid.

24. Joe Califano, *How to Raise a Drug-Free Kid: The Straight Dope for Parents* (New York: Simon & Schuster, 2014), 45–46.

25. "Chronic Marijuana Smoking Affects Brain Chemistry, Molecular Imaging Shows": http://www.sciencedaily.com/releases/2011/06/110606131705.htm

26. "The Squeaky Wheel": http://www.psychologytoday.com/blog/the-squeaky -wheel/201208/study-finds-regular-marijuana-use-damages-teenage-brains

27. "Cannabis: A Danger to the Adolescent Brain—How Pediatricians Can Address Marijuana Use": http://www.mcpap.com/pdf/Cannibis.pdf
28. "Is Super Weed, Super Bad?": http://www.cnn.com/2013/08/09/health/weed-potency-levels/
29. Ibid.
30. "Cannabis Use in Teens Linked to Irreparable Drop in IQ": http://www.medscape.com/viewarticle/803197
31. "Early Marijuana Use Linked to I.Q. Loss": http://well.blogs.nytimes.com/2012/08/27/early-marijuana-use-linked-to-to-i-q-loss
32. Jerome M. Sattler, *Assessment of Children: Cognitive Foundations* (La Mesa, CA: Jerome M. Sattler, 2008).
33. "Marijuana IQ Study Successfully Defended by Scientists": http://www.cadca.org/resources/detail/marijuana-iq-study-successfully-defended-scientists
34. "Merck Yanks Vioxx From Shelves": http://www.cbsnews.com/news/merck-yanks-vioxx-from-shelves/
35. "Thalidomide, Long Banned, Wins Support": http://www.nytimes.com/1997/09/06/us/thalidomide-long-banned-wins-support.html
36. He has since been approved and sworn into office.
37. "Senate Panel Considers Nominee to Head Safety Commission": http://wabe.org/post/senate-panel-considers-obama-nominee-head-safety-commission
38. "Report to Congress on the Prevention and Reduction of Underage Drinking": https://store.samhsa.gov/shin/content/PEP13-RTCUAD/PEP13-RTCUAD.pdf
39. "Youth and Tobacco Use": http://www.cdc.gov/tobacco/data_statistics/fact_sheets/youth_data/tobacco_use/
40. "The Right Drug to Target": http://www.washingtonpost.com/wp-dyn/content/article/2005/05/17/AR2005051700876.html
41. "The Teen Brain on Marijuana": http://www.ceasar-boston.org/about/TeenBrainandMj2012.pdf
42. Ibid.
43. "Marijuana Users Have Abnormal Brain Structure and Poor Memory": http://www.northwestern.edu/newscenter/stories/2013/12/marijuana-users-have-abnormal-brain-structure--poor-memory.html
44. Ibid.
45. "Driving Under the Influence, of Marijuana": http://www.nytimes.com/2014/02/18/health/driving-under-the-influence-of-marijuana.html
46. "DrugFacts: Marijuana": http://www.drugabuse.gov/publications/drugfacts/marijuana
47. "Potential for Heart Attack, Stroke Risk Seen with Marijuana Use": http://www.latimes.com/science/sciencenow/la-sci-sn-heart-attack-stroke-marijuana-20140423-story.html

48. "The Good, the Bud and the Ugly: What 20 Years of Research Teaches Us About Cannabis": http://www.newsweek.com/good-bud-and-ugly-what -20-years-cannabis-research-teaches-us-275979

49. "What Has Research Over the Past Two Decades Revealed About the Adverse Health Effects of Recreational Cannabis Use?": http://onlinelibrary.wiley.com/ enhanced/doi/10.1111/add.12703/

Chapter 2: What Is "Medical Marijuana"?

1. Minnesota also allows medical marijuana, but prohibits patients from smoking the drug.

2. "Amsterdam for Tourists: What's Legal?": http://www.cnn.com/2013/07/17/ travel/amsterdam-travel-legal-parameters/

3. "Eric Holder 'Cautiously Optimistic' About Marijuana Legalization": http:// www.msnbc.com/msnbc/cautiously-optimistic-about-legal-weed

4. "Fox 5 Proves Medical Marijuana Card 'Easy' to Get": http://fox5sandiego .com/2013/04/25/fox-5-proves-medical-marijuana-card-easy-to-get/

5. "Conditions That Qualify for Medical Marijuana Card in California": https:// www.unitedpatientsgroup.com/blog/2012/02/15/conditions-that-qualify-for -medical-marijuana-card-in-california/

6. "Medical Marijuana Program Is a Charade": http://archive.azcentral.com/ members/Blog/LaurieRoberts/174454

7. Ibid.

8. "Don't Go to Pot": http://www.commentarymagazine.com/article/dont-go -to-pot/

9. "Marijuana Testing Labs Barred from Taking Samples from Individuals": http://www.denverpost.com/marijuana/ci_25688115/marijuana-testing-labs -barred-from-taking-samples-from

10. Ibid.

11. "11 Facts About Teens and Drug Use": https://www.dosomething.org/facts/ 11-facts-about-teens-and-drug-use

12. "Substance Abuse Treatment Admissions Aged 15 to 17": http://www.samhsa .gov/data/2k12/TEDS_061/TEDS_061_LateAdolescents_2012.htm

13. Ibid.

14. "Marijuana Playing Larger Role in Fatal Crashes": http://www.usatoday.com/ story/money/cars/2014/06/09/marijuana-accidents/10219119

15. Ibid.

16. "In Past Decade, Traffic Fatalities Involving Marijuana Have Spiked": http:// dailysignal.com/2014/06/11/past-decade-traffic-fatalities-involving -marijuana-spiked

17. "The Myths of Smoking Pot": http://www.washingtonpost.com/opinions/ ruth-marcus-national-institute-on-drug-abuse-chief-attacks-myths-of-pot -smoking/2014/06/24/12010d84-fbd9-11e3-8176-f2c941cf35f1_story.html

18. EPIC was established by the federal government in 1974 to assist in the identification of drug and alien traffickers. It is currently run jointly by the DEA and Customs and Border Protection (CBP), and provides assistance to federal, state, and local law enforcement authorities.

19. "Increasing Numbers of Dogs Ingesting Marijuana": http://www.redorbit.com/ news/science/1113051911/marijuana-poisoning-on-the-rise-in-pets-012214/

20. "More Arizona Dogs Getting Sick Eating Edible Pot": http://tucson.com/news/ state-and-regional/more-arizona-dogs-getting-sick-eating-edible-pot/article _aa72b665-db11-52d4-a90f-079bac30bf6d.html

21. Ibid.

22. "Colorado Study Warns of Dangers of Children Accidentally Ingesting Medical Marijuana": http://www.boston.com/whitecoatnotes/blogs/white-coat -notes/2013/05/27/colorado-study-warns-dangers-children-accidentally -ingesting-medical-marijuana/Y0idWScxyeMRUKXPIGOI1K/story.html

23. Ibid.

24. Ibid.

25. "What Is Cannabis?": http://learnaboutmarijuanawa.org/factsheets/whatis cannabis.htm

26. "The Myths of Smoking Pot": http://www.washingtonpost.com/opinions/ ruth-marcus-national-institute-on-drug-abuse-chief-attacks-myths-of -pot-smoking/2014/06/24/12010d84-fbd9-11e3-8176-f2c941cf35f1_story.html

27. "Denver Now Has More Marijuana Dispensaries Than It Does Starbucks": http://www.huffingtonpost.com/2011/07/06/medical-marijuana-denver -starbucks_n_891796.html

28. "The Legalization of Marijuana in Colorado: The Impact": http://www.rmhidta .org/html/FINAL%20Legalization%20of%20MJ%20in%20Colorado%20 The%20Impact.pdf

29. "California Dispensaries Outnumber Starbucks & McDonald's 2:1": http:// theopenend.com/2009/08/12/california-dispensaries-outnumber-starbucks -mcdonalds-21/

30. *Phoenix New Times*, February 27–March 5, 2014, 60–69.

31. "Colorado Dispensary Sales Soar 50%, Hit $329M": http://mmjbusinessdaily .com/329m-medical-marijuana-market-in-colorado/

32. "23 Legal Medical Marijuana States and DC": http://medicalmarijuana.procon .org/view.resource.php?resourceID=000881

33. "10 Things to Know About Nation's First Recreational Marijuana Shops in Colorado": http://www.cnn.com/2013/12/28/us/10-things-colorado-recreational -marijuana/

34. "Position Statement on Marijuana as Medicine": http://www.psych.org/advocacy —newsroom/position-statements

35. "Medical Marijuana: Public Policy Statement on Medical Marijuana": http://www.asam.org/advocacy/find-a-policy-statement/view-policy-statement/ public-policy-statements/2011/12/15/medical-marijuana

36. "Medical Use of Marijuana: ACS Position": http://medicalmarijuana.procon.org/ sourcefiles/american-cancer-society-position.pdf

37. "Position Statement on Marijuana and the Treatment of Glaucoma": http:// www.americanglaucomasociety.net/patients/position_statements/marijuana _glaucoma

38. "Legalization of Marijuana: Potential Impact on Youth": http://pediatrics .aappublications.org/content/113/6/1825.full.pdf

39. *The Giving Tree of Denver*: http://www.tgtree.com/games-giveaways/

40. Tauheed Zaman, M.D., Richard N. Rosenthal, M.D., John A. Renner, Jr., M.D., Herbert D. Kleber, M.D., Robert Milin, M.D., "Resource Document on Marijuana as Medicine," American Psychiatric Association.

41. "Psychiatrist Claims Medical Marijuana Dangerous for Treatment of Psychiatric Problems": http://www.news-medical.net/news/20130122/Psychiatrist -claims-medical-marijuana-dangerous-for-treatment-of-psychiatric-problems .aspx

42. "Why I Would Vote No on Pot": http://www.cannabisculture.com/why-i-would -vote-no-on-pot

43. "Why I Changed My Mind on Weed": http://www.cnn.com/2013/08/08/health/ gupta-changed-mind-marijuana/

44. Ibid.

45. "Charlotte Figi: The Girl Who Is Changing Medical Marijuana Laws Across America": http://www.ibtimes.co.uk/charlotte-figi-girl-who-changing-medical -marijuana-laws-across-america-1453547

46. *Helping Hands Herbals*: http://helpinghandsdispensary.com/

47. "Fox News Poll: 85 Percent of Voters Favor Medical Marijuana": http://www .foxnews.com/politics/interactive/2013/05/01/fox-news-poll-85-percent -voters-favor-medical-marijuana/

48. "Medical Marijuana: The Institute of Medicine Report": http://www .psychiatrictimes.com/articles/medical-marijuana-institute-medicine-report

49. Ibid.

50. "Problems with the Medicalization of Marijuana": http://jama.jamanetwork
    .com/article.aspx?articleID=1874073
51. Ibid.
52. Ibid.
53. "Does the Pot Pill Work?": http://www.cbsnews.com/news/does-the-pot-pill
    -work/
54. "Problems with the Medicalization of Marijuana": http://jama.jamanetwork
    .com/article.aspx?articleID=1874073
55. "Laetrile/Amygdalin (PDQ®)": http://www.cancer.gov/cancertopics/pdq/cam/
    laetrile/HealthProfessional/page2
56. "The Laetrile Scam: Testimonials Are Not Science": http://alternative-doctor
    .com/cancer_therapies/laetrile-scam/
57. "NORML and the Scam of Medical Marijuana / Anti-Marijuana Video":
    https://www.youtube.com/watch?v=ccjLM4-4U2k

Chapter 3: Legalization and Its Effects

1. "Speaking Out Against Drug Legalization": http://www.justice.gov/dea/pr/
   multimedia-library/publications/speaking_out.pdf
2. "Alaska Marijuana Criminalization Initiative (1990)": http://ballotpedia.org/
   Alaska_Marijuana_Criminalization_Initiative_%281990%29
3. "Alaska Marijuana Decriminalization Initiative, Measure 5 (2000)": http://
   ballotpedia.org/Alaska_Marijuana_Decriminalization_Initiative,_Measure_5
   _%282000%29
4. "Timeline: Notable Moments in 40 Years of Alaska's History with Marijuana":
   http://www.alaskadispatch.com/article/20140413/timeline-notable-moments
   -40-years-alaskas-history-marijuana
5. "Don't Harsh Our Mellow, Dude": http://www.nytimes.com/2014/06/04/
   opinion/dowd-dont-harsh-our-mellow-dude.html
6. Ibid.
7. Ibid.
8. "Why Eating a Marijuana Candy Bar Sent Maureen Dowd to Paranoia Hell":
   http://www.forbes.com/sites/daviddisalvo/2014/06/09/why-eating-a-marijuana
   -candy-bar-sent-maureen-dowd-to-paranoia-hell/
9. "Going to Pot?": http://www.slate.com/articles/news_and_politics/politics/
   2014/05/colorado_s_pot_experiment_the_unintended_consequences_of
   _marijuana_legalization.html
10. Ibid.

11. Ibid.
12. "Don't Harsh Our Mellow, Dude": http://www.nytimes.com/2014/06/04/opinion/dowd-dont-harsh-our-mellow-dude.html
13. "After 5 Months of Sales, Colorado Sees the Downside of a Legal High": http://www.nytimes.com/2014/06/01/us/after-5-months-of-sales-colorado-sees-the-downside-of-a-legal-high.html
14. Ibid.
15. "DUI Admissions to Arapahoe House Detox Facilities Involving Marijuana Nearly Double Since Legalization": https://www.arapahoehouse.org/dui-admissions-arapahoe-house-detox-facilities-involving-marijuana-nearly-double-legalization
16. "Six Months Into Colorado Weed Experiment": http://www.cnn.com/video/data/2.0/video/us/2014/06/30/orig-jql-colorado-marijuana-six-month-anniversary-ana-cabrera.cnn.html
17. "Colorado Governor: Cannabis Legalization Was 'Reckless'": http://www.businessinsider.com/governor-of-colorado-cannabis-legalization-was-reckless-2014-10
18. "Physicians and Medical Marijuana": http://ajp.psychiatryonline.org/article.aspx?articleid=1170852
19. "Obama Jokes White House Pastry Chef Puts Crack in His Pies": http://www.breitbart.com/Breitbart-TV/2014/06/30/Obama-Jokes-White-House-Pastry-Chef-Puts-Crack-In-His-Pies
20. "The Public Health Consequences of Marijuana Legalization": http://www.whitehouse.gov/sites/default/files/ondcp/issues-content/marijuana_and_public_health_one_pager_-_final.pdf
21. Mark A. R. Kleiman, Jonathan P. Caulkins, Angela Hawken, *Drugs and Drug Policy: What Everyone Needs to Know* (New York: Oxford University Press, 2011), 29–30.
22. Ibid., 25.

Chapter 4: Drug War Myths

1. "Sensible on Weed": http://www.nationalreview.com/article/367618/sensible-weed-editors
2. Ibid.
3. Ibid.
4. "Size of Colorado Pot Demand? Try 130 Metric Tons": http://www.cnbc.com/id/101826910.

5. "Study: Fatal Car Crashes Involving Marijuana Have Tripled": http://seattle .cbslocal.com/2014/02/04/study-fatal-car-crashes-involving-marijuana-have -tripled/

6. "Two Denver Deaths Tied to Recreational Marijuana Use": http://www .cbsnews.com/news/two-denver-deaths-tied-to-recreational-marijuana-use/

7. "Police: Student Ate Too Much Marijuana Cookie Before Fatal Jump": http:// www.komonews.com/news/national/Police-Student-ate-more-pot-than -recommended-before-fatal-jump-255715881.html

8. "Cerebellar Infarction in Adolescent Males Associated with Acute Marijuana Use": http://pediatrics.aappublications.org/content/113/4/e365.full

9. "Acute Cardiovascular Fatalities Following Cannabis Use": http://www .fsijournal.org/article/S0379-0738%2801%2900609-0/abstract

10. "Comparing Alcohol and Marijuana: Seriously": http://www.hudson.org/ research/10478-comparing-alcohol-and-marijuana-seriously

11. "DrugFacts: Drugged Driving": http://www.drugabuse.gov/publications/ drugfacts/drugged-driving

12. "Driving Under the Influence, of Marijuana": http://www.nytimes.com/2014/ 02/18/health/driving-under-the-influence-of-marijuana.html

13. "More Teens Seek Marijuana Addiction Treatment": http://www.mainstreet .com/article/more-teens-seek-marijuana-addiction-treatment

14. "New Studies Show Long-Term Effects of Cannabis on the Brain": http://blogs .psychcentral.com/science-addiction/2014/04/new-studies-show-long-term -effects-of-cannabis-on-the-brain/

15. "The War on Marijuana In Black and White": http://www.aclu.org/files/assets/ aclu-thewaronmarijuana-rel2.pdf

16. "UN 101: What the U.S. Pays the U.N.": http://www.humanrightsvoices.org/ EYEontheUN/un_101/facts/?p=15

17. "Warren Buffett Made $1 Billion in First 22 Hours of March Madness": http:// www.forbes.com/sites/danalexander/2014/03/21/warren-buffett-had-already -made-1-billion-22-hours-into-march-madness/

18. "Summaries of Fiscal Year 2013 Proposed Executive Budgets": http://www .nasbo.org/summaries_FY2013_proposed_budgets

19. "Marijuana: Pot Prohibition Costs $41 Billion a Year in Enforcement Costs, Lost Tax Revenues, Study Finds": http://stopthedrugwar.org/chronicle/2007/ oct/05/marijuana_pot_prohibition_costs

20. "The Price of Legalizing Pot Is Too High": http://articles.latimes.com/2009/ jun/07/opinion/oe-sabet7

21. "Top 10 Marijuana Myths and Facts": http://www.rollingstone.com/culture/ lists/top-10-marijuana-myths-and-facts-20120822/myth-prisons-are-full -of-people-in-for-marijuana-possession-19691231

22. Ibid.
23. "Drunk Driving by the Numbers": http://www.rita.dot.gov/bts/sites/rita.dot
    .gov.bts/files/publications/by_the_numbers/drunk_driving/index.html
24. "Uniform Crime Reports: Crime in the United States 2011": http://www
    .fbi.gov/about-us/cjis/ucr/crime-in-the-u.s/2011/crime-in-the-u.s.-2011/
    persons-arrested/persons-arrested/
25. "7 Big Myths About Marijuana and Legalization": http://www.csmonitor.com/
    Commentary/Opinion/2013/0905/7-big-myths-about-marijuana-and
    -legalization/Myth-Countless-people-are-behind-bars-simply-for-smoking
    -marijuana
26. "Marijuana Myths & Facts: The Truth Behind 10 Popular Misperceptions":
    https://www.ncjrs.gov/ondcppubs/publications/pdf/marijuana_myths_facts.pdf
27. "Marijuana and Punishment: Debunking Pot Proponents' Prison Myths":
    http://sjipc.org/marijuana-and-punishment-debunking-pot-proponents-prison
    -myths-by-michael-p-tremoglie/
28. "Altered State?: Assessing How Marijuana Legalization in California Could
    Influence Marijuana Consumption and Public Budgets": http://www.rand.org/
    content/dam/rand/pubs/occasional_papers/2010/RAND_OP315.pdf
29. Ibid.
30. Ibid.
31. Sheila Polk, "What If…Marijuana Was Legal in Arizona for Recreational
    Purposes," *Arizona Republic*, April 20, 2014.
32. "Where Does Pot Come From: Domestic Growers or Mexican Cartels?": http://
    www.fronterasdesk.org/content/where-does-pot-come-domestic-growers-or
    -mexican-cartels
33. "Mexican Drug Cartels Outgunning Law Enforcement Across the U.S.—Not
    Just Near the Border—and Have Infiltrated 3,000 Cities, Sheriffs Warn":
    http://www.dailymail.co.uk/news/article-2603819/Mexican-drug-cartels
    -outgunning-law-enforcement-U-S-not-just-near-border-infiltrated-3-000
    -cities-sheriffs-warn.html
34. "DEA: Drug Cartels Look to Capitalize on Legal Marijuana Laws": http://
    www.washingtontimes.com/news/2014/mar/4/dea-drug-cartels-look-to
    -capitalize-on-legal-marij/?page=all
35. "Drug Cartels Muscle in to Piracy Business": http://www.washingtonpost
    .com/world/americas/drug-cartels-muscle-in-to-piracy-business/2011/05/28/
    AG93GLEH_story.html
36. "Colorado Pot Shops Likely Targets of Cartels, Say Experts": http://www
    .foxnews.com/us/2014/01/11/colorado-pot-shops-likely-targets-cartels-say
    -experts/

37. "Denver DA's Version of Violent Medical Marijuana Industry Questioned": http://www.denverpost.com/breakingnews/ci_23763821/denver-das-version -violent-medical-marijuana-industry-questioned

38. "Crimes at Medical Marijuana Dispensaries Raise Security Concerns": http://www.myfoxphoenix.com/story/19930015/2012/10/27/crimes-at-medical -marijuana-dispensaries-raise-concerns

39. "Colorado Pot Shops Likely Targets of Cartels, Say Experts": http://www.fox news.com/us/2014/01/11/colorado-pot-shops-likely-targets-cartels-say-experts/

40. "Reducing Drug Trafficking Revenues and Violence in Mexico: Would Legalizing Marijuana in California Help?": http://www.rand.org/content/dam/ rand/pubs/occasional_papers/2010/RAND_OP325.pdf

41. Ibid.

42. "Study: California Legalizing Pot Won't Hinder Mexican Cartels": http:// sanfrancisco.cbslocal.com/2010/10/12/study-california-legalizing-pot-wont -hinder-mexican-cartels/

43. "Cigarette Taxes and Cigarette Smuggling by State": http://taxfoundation.org/ article/cigarette-taxes-and-cigarette-smuggling-state

44. Ibid.

45. "Medical Marijuana Statistics": https://www.colorado.gov/pacific/cdphe/medical -marijuana-statistics

46. Sheila Polk, "What If…Marijuana Was Legal in Arizona for Recreational Purposes," *Arizona Republic*, April 20, 2014.

47. "Legalize Pot? No, Reform Laws": http://www.cnn.com/2012/11/20/opinion/ sabet-marijuana-legalization/

48. "Tobacco Tax Revenue": http://www.taxpolicycenter.org/taxfacts/displayafact .cfm?Docid=403

49. "Stairway to Recovery": http://www.uphs.upenn.edu/addiction/berman/society/ econ.html

50. "Tax Facts: Alcohol Tax Revenue": http://www.taxpolicycenter.org/taxfacts/ displayafact.cfm?Docid=399

51. "Recreational Pot Not Bringing in Tax Money That Was Expected": http:// denver.cbslocal.com/2014/09/02/recreational-pot-not-bringing-in-tax-money -that-was-expected/

52. In trying to reach a consensus about the number of dollars generated for the State of Colorado, our own research and discussions with the Department of Revenue put the number in the low $20 million range.

53. "Marijuana Revenue Still Hazy for States": http://www.pewtrusts.org/en/ research-and-analysis/blogs/stateline/2014/09/16/marijuana-revenue-still -hazy-for-states

54. "Hickenlooper: I Hate This Experiment": http://durangoherald.com/article/
    20140110/NEWS01/140119986/Hickenlooper:-I-hate-this-experiment
55. Daniel Okrent, *Last Call: The Rise and Fall of Prohibition* (New York: Scribner,
    2011), 373.
56. "Actually, Prohibition Was a Success": http://www.nytimes.com/1989/10/16/
    opinion/actually-prohibition-was-a-success.html

Chapter 5: How the Culture Once Successfully Fought Back on Substance Abuse

1. "Nine Terrifying Facts About America's Biggest Police Force": http://www
   .salon.com/2012/09/28/nine_terrifying_facts_about_americas_biggest_police
   _force/
2. "Substance Use and Mental Health Estimates from the 2013 National Survey
   on Drug Use and Health: Overview of Findings": http://www.samhsa.gov/
   data/sites/default/files/NSDUH-SR200-RecoveryMonth-2014/NSDUH-SR200
   -RecoveryMonth-2014.htm
3. Ibid.
4. "Drug Use Trends": http://www.policyalmanac.org/crime/archive/drug_use
   _trends.shtml
5. "DrugFacts: Nationwide Trends": http://www.drugabuse.gov/publications/
   drugfacts/nationwide-trends
6. Kevin Sabet, *Reefer Sanity: Seven Great Myths About Marijuana* (New York:
   Beaufort Books, 2013).
7. "'Weeds' Sets Showtime Ratings Record": http://www.hollywoodreporter
   .com/news/weeds-sets-showtime-ratings-record-113998
8. "WH Report: Chronic Marijuana Users Up 84% in 10 Years": http://cnsnews
   .com/news/article/ali-meyer/wh-report-chronic-marijuana-users-84-10-years
9. Ibid.

Chapter 6: The International Experience

1. "Is Cannabis Legal in The Netherlands?": http://www.dailysmoker.com/
   various/amsterdam/drug-policy/cannabis-legal-netherlands
2. "Teenage Cannabis Addiction on the Rise": http://www.rnw.nl/english/article/
   teenage-cannabis-addiction-rise
3. "Dutch Classify High-Potency Marijuana as Hard Drug": http://www.foxnews
   .com/world/2011/10/07/dutch-classify-high-potency-marijuana-as-hard-drug/

4. "What Can We Learn from the Dutch Cannabis Coffeeshop Experience?": http://www.rand.org/content/dam/rand/pubs/working_papers/2010/RAND _WR768.pdf
5. Ibid.
6. Ibid.
7. "Amsterdam Crackdown on Marijuana Cafes": http://www.stuff.co.nz/world/ europe/9972625/Amsterdam-crackdown-on-marijuana-cafes
8. "While U.S. States Relax Marijuana Laws, Pot Haven Netherlands Cracks Down, with Mixed Success": http://www.cbsnews.com/news/while-us-states -relax-marijuana-laws-pot-haven-netherlands-cracks-down-with-mixed -success/
9. *INCB Report 2013*, "Chapter III. Analysis of the World Situation": http:// www.incb.org/documents/Publications/AnnualReports/AR2013/English/AR _2013_E_Chapter_III.pdf
10. "Getting a Fix": http://www.newyorker.com/reporting/2011/10/17/111017fa _fact_specter
11. Ibid.
12. "Portugal 2013 Crime and Safety Report": https://www.osac.gov/pages/ ContentReportDetails.aspx?cid=13669
13. "Drug Decriminalization in Portugal: Challenges and Limitations": http:// www.whitehouse.gov/sites/default/files/ondcp/Fact_Sheets/portugal_fact _sheet_8-25-10.pdf
14. Ibid.
15. "Decriminalisation of Drugs in Portugal Was Not a Success, Says Dr. Manuel Pinto Coelho": http://www.huffingtonpost.co.uk/2012/12/10/portugal -decriminalisation-drugs-britain_n_2270789.html
16. "Uruguay Has Big Hopes for Pot Industry": http://online.wsj.com/news/ articles/SB10001424052702304422704579571910719025796
17. "Uruguay Marijuana Laws Banned by UN": http://449recovery.org/blog/ uruguay-marijuana-laws-banned-un/
18. "Why Brazil Is Not Cool with Uruguay's Legalization of Marijuana": http:// www.worldcrunch.com/world-affairs/why-brazil-is-not-cool-with-uruguay -039-s-legalization-of-marijuana/cannabis-drug-legalization-prevention/ c1s14508/#.U4Nwwi_D87A
19. "'First Ever' Bill Proposes Legal Cannabis in France": http://www.thelocal .fr/20140130/frances-first-law-to-re
20. "Know Your Limit: Germany Seeks Uniform Law on Marijuana": http:// www.spiegel.de/international/germany/german-states-consider-standardizing -marijuana-rules-a-901717.html

21. "Poll Stubs Out Legal Cannabis Hopes": http://www.thelocal.de/20140109/poll-stubs-out-cannabis-cafe-hopes

22. "Drug Laws in Singapore": http://goseasia.about.com/od/singapore/a/Singapore-Drug-Laws.htm

23. "20 Years After Pablo: The Evolution of Colombia's Drug Trade": http://www.insightcrime.org/news-analysis/20-years-after-pablo-the-evolution-of-colombias-drug-trade

24. "Black Market Weed Rampant on Colorado Public Land": http://www.mainstreet.com/article/black-market-weed-rampant-colorado-public-land

25. Ibid.

26. "Marijuana Legalization Won't Crowd Out Cartels": http://dailycaller.com/2014/05/21/marijuana-legalization-wont-crowd-out-cartels/

27. Ibid.

28. "Cannabis: An Apology": http://www.independent.co.uk/life-style/health-and-families/health-news/cannabis-an-apology-440730.html

29. *INCB Report 2013*, "Chapter III. Analysis of the World Situation": http://www.incb.org/documents/Publications/AnnualReports/AR2013/English/AR_2013_E_Chapter_III.pdf

30. Ibid.

31. *INCB Report 2013*, "Chapter 1. Economic Consequences of Drug Abuse": http://www.incb.org/documents/Publications/AnnualReports/AR2013/English/AR_2013_E_Chapter_I.pdf

Chapter 7: How to Answer Legalization Efforts and Argue with Those Who Support Legalization

1. "CNN Poll: Support for Legal Marijuana Soaring": http://politicalticker.blogs.cnn.com/2014/01/06/cnn-poll-support-for-legal-marijuana-soaring/

2. Ibid.

3. Cambridge Study Center: http://www.cambridgestudycenter.com/quotes/authors/flannery-o-connor/

4. "Marijuana Use and Risk of Lung Cancer: A 40-Year Cohort Study": http://www.ncbi.nlm.nih.gov/pubmed/23846283

5. "Does the Regular Smoking of Marijuana Cause Lung Cancer or in Any Way Permanently Injure the Lungs?": http://medicalmarijuana.procon.org/view.answers.php?questionID=000234

6. "Study: Pot Increases Heart Attack Risks": http://abcnews.go.com/Health/story?id=117399

7. "Marijuana Linked to Heart Problems": http://www.newsday.com/news/health/marijuana-linked-to-heart-problems-1.7836745
8. Ibid.
9. "The Cannabis-Psychosis Link": http://www.psychiatrictimes.com/schizophrenia/cannabis-psychosis-link/page/0/2#sthash.gEEt6Pni.dpuf
10. "Marijuana May Hurt the Developing Teen Brain": http://www.npr.org/blogs/health/2014/02/25/282631913/marijuana-may-hurt-the-developing-teen-brain
11. "Mental Health and Marijuana": http://adai.uw.edu/marijuana/factsheets/mentalhealth.htm
12. "Is Marijuana Addictive?": http://www.psychologytoday.com/blog/almost-addicted/201311/is-marijuana-addictive
13. "Is Marijuana Addictive? It Depends How You Define Addiction": http://healthland.time.com/2010/10/19/is-marijuana-addictive-it-depends-how-you-define-addiction/
14. "Clinical Trial Testing New Treatment for Marijuana Addiction": http://www.greenvilleonline.com/story/news/2014/02/27/clinical-trial-testing-new-treatment-for-marijuana-addiction/5869119/
15. "DrugFacts: Nationwide Trends": http://www.drugabuse.gov/publications/drugfacts/nationwide-trends
16. Ibid.
17. Sheila Polk, "What If...Marijuana Was Legal in Arizona for Recreational Purposes," *Arizona Republic*, April 20, 2014.
18. "Colo. Teen Addiction Centers Gear Up for Legal Pot": http://abcnews.go.com/blogs/health/2014/01/03/colo-teen-addiction-centers-gear-up-for-legal-pot/
19. "Ledger Enjoyed the Weed, a Lot": http://radaronline.com/exclusives/2008/10/heath-ledger-used-to-like-smoking-pot-a-lot-php/
20. "Whitney Houston Was 'Winning Battle Against Drugs Hell'": http://www.mirror.co.uk/news/world-news/whitney-houston-was-winning-battle-against-682701
21. "'Glee' Star Monteith Opens Up About Drug Abuse": http://www.today.com/id/43512715/ns/today-today_entertainment/t/glee-star-monteith-opens-about-drug-abuse/
22. "Genius, But Amy's Was Not a Life to Admire": http://www.dailymail.co.uk/debate/article-2018741/Amy-Winehouse-dead-Genius-life-admire.html
23. Kevin Sabet, *Reefer Sanity: Seven Great Myths About Marijuana* (New York: Beaufort Books, 2013).
24. "Police: Drug Arrests Connected to Hoffman Death Investigation": http://abcnews.go.com/Entertainment/police-hoffmans-heroin-didnt-additive-death-investigation-continues/story?id=22370240

25. "Yale Study: Marijuana May Really Be Gateway Drug": http://www.ctpost .com/local/article/Yale-study-Marijuana-may-really-be-gateway-drug -3805532.php

26. "Myth: Marijuana Is Harmless": http://alcoholism.about.com/od/pot/a/bldea 050426_4.htm

27. "CVS to Stop Selling Cigarettes": http://online.wsj.com/news/articles/SB10001 424052702304851104579363520905849600

28. Ibid.

29. "If Marijuana Is Legalized, Who Will Start Using More of It?": http://www .theatlantic.com/health/archive/2013/07/if-marijuana-is-legalized-who -will-start-using-more-of-it/277686/

30. "4th-Graders Sell Pot in Northern Colo.": http://www.foxnews.com/us/2014 /04/23/4th-grader-sells-pot-in-northern-colorado/

31. "Altered State?: Assessing How Marijuana Legalization in California Could Influence Marijuana Consumption and Public Budgets": http://www.rand.org/ pubs/occasional_papers/OP315.html

32. "Let States Decide on Pot": http://www.nationalreview.com/article/379018/ let-states-decide-pot-dana-rohrabacher

33. Ibid.

34. Google search results: https://www.google.com/search?q=prescription+drug+ epidemic&ie=utf-8&oe=utf-8&aq=t&rls=org.mozilla:en-US:official&client =firefox-a&channel=fflb

35. "Let States Decide on Pot": http://www.nationalreview.com/article/379018/ let-states-decide-pot-dana-rohrabacher

36. U.S. Food and Drug Administration, "About the FDA": http://www.fda.gov/ aboutfda/whatwedo/history/default.htm

37. "Gonzales V. Raich (03-1454) 545 U.S. 1 (2005) 352 F.3d 1222, vacated and remanded": http://www.law.cornell.edu/supct/html/03-1454.ZC.html

38. "The Legalization of Marijuana in Colorado: The Impact": http://www.rmhidta .org/html/FINAL%20Legalization%20of%20MJ%20in%20Colorado%20 The%20Impact.pdf

39. "The Partial Birth Abortion Ban": http://archive.lewrockwell.com/paul/ paul98.html

40. Jonathan P. Caulkins, Angela Hawken, Beau Kilmer, Mark A. R. Kleiman, *Marijuana Legalization: What Everyone Needs to Know* (New York: Oxford University Press, 2012).

41. Ibid.

Chapter 8: Conclusion

1. Jonathan P. Caulkins, Angela Hawken, Beau Kilmer, Mark Kleiman, *Marijuana Legalization: What Everyone Needs to Know* (New York: Oxford University Press, 2012), 135.
2. Mark A. R. Kleiman, Jonathan P. Caulkins, Angela Hawken, *Drugs and Drug Policy: What Everyone Needs to Know* (New York: Oxford University Press, 2011).
3. "This Is Your Brain on Drugs": http://www.nytimes.com/2014/11/02/education/edlife/this-is-your-brain-on-drugs-marijuana-adults-teens.html
4. "After 5 Months of Sales, Colorado Sees the Downside of a Legal High": http://www.nytimes.com/2014/06/01/us/after-5-months-of-sales-colorado-sees-the-downside-of-a-legal-high.html
5. "Pot Seen as Reason for Rise in Denver Homeless": http://news.yahoo.com/pot-seen-reason-rise-denver-homeless-175115981.html?soc_src=mediacontentsharebuttons
6. "Legal Pot Drives Up Number of Homeless in Denver": http://www.nydailynews.com/news/national/legal-pot-raises-homeless-numbers-denver-article-1.1881281
7. "My Dad Will Never Stop Smoking Pot": http://www.theatlantic.com/health/archive/2014/01/my-dad-will-never-stop-smoking-pot/283085/
8. Jonathan P. Caulkins, Angela Hawken, Beau Kilmer, Mark A. R. Kleiman, *Marijuana Legalization: What Everyone Needs to Know* (New York: Oxford University Press, 2012).

Index

Index

Index

Index

Index

anti-cigarette ads, 9
medical marijuana, 31, 36–37, 44, 50
Arizona Daily Star, 44
Arizona Republic, 36
arrests for marijuana, 95–100, 104, 168–69
interdiction seizures, 42–43, *43,* 161–62
Association for a Drug Free Portugal, 132
Atlantic (magazine), 175–77
attitudes toward marijuana, xviii, 10–12,
116–17, 177–78
drug use and stigmatization, 7–10
Hollywood's role, 117–18, 119–23
polling data, xvi–xvii, 142–43
President Obama and, 2–3, 116–17
Attorney General of the United States,
32–33, 67
auto accidents/deaths, and marijuana use,
26–27, 28, 74–75, 87, 88, 92, 141,
166, 176, 184–85

Baler, Ruben, 181–92
Big Marijuana, 79–81
Big Tobacco, 79, 81
black markets and sumptuary laws,
100–104
Boston Children's Hospital, 25–26
Botticelli, Michael, 117
Boyd, Wes, 147
brain (brain development), adverse effects
of marijuana use, 20–23, 147, 183
adolescent brain, xiii, 15–17, 58–59, 92,
172–73
judgment, coordination and motor
skills, 26–27
brain safety, and football helmets, 23–24
Bratton, William, 124*n*
Brazil, 134
"broken windows" theory, 124, 124*n*
Brown, Jerry, xix, 6
Buckley, William F., Jr., 84–85, 86
Bush, George H. W., 2, 116–17
butane hash oil (BHO), 73–74

Califano, Joe, 15, 157, 174
California
marijuana arrests, 100
marijuana legalization, 10,
102–3, 156

medical marijuana, xvii–xviii, 30–31,
37, 50
states' rights arguments, 158–59, 162
cancer
Laetrile, 69
marijuana and adverse effects, 13, 14,
55, 146, 185
medical marijuana for, 36, 37, 62,
178
Cannabis Cup, 18
car accidents. *See* auto accidents/deaths,
and marijuana use
cardiovascular health, adverse effects of
marijuana use on, 27–29, 91–92,
146–47
cartels and legalization, 100–104
Caulkins, Jonathan P., 80–81, 96, 164–65,
170, 179
children
access to medical marijuana, 37–39
adverse effects of marijuana use on
brain, xiii, 15–17, 58–59, 92,
172–73
anti-drug ads, 116
marijuana legalization and its effects on,
70, 73, 74–75, 168, 174
marketing of medical marijuana in
Colorado, 46–48
parent-pot chic, 10–11
chronic pain, medical marijuana
for, 36
cigarettes (tobacco), 145–46, 156–57
addiction to, 79, 147–48
black market, 103
costs vs. tax revenues, 104–5
CVS sales, 155
hypothetical legalization argument,
xv–xvi
industry profits and heavy users, 79
marijuana compared with, 48–49,
104–5, 145–46, 155, 156–57
marketing of, 19, 48–49
stigmatization of, 8–9, 118
teen use, 8, 24–25, 48–49
cocaine, 7, 47*n,* 132, 136, 140, 147, 150,
154
Coelho, Manuel Pinto, 132
Colombia, 135–36

212

Index

Colorado
banking rules, 101–2
black market sales of marijuana, 103–4
marijuana interdiction seizures, 42–44,
43, 161–62
marijuana legalization, xviii, 10, 32,
39–40, 71–72, 148–49
homelessness, 174–75
interstate consequences, 42–43, *43,*
86–88
political debate and states' rights
arguments, 83, 85, 86–87, 160,
161–62
tax revenues, 103–4, 107, 203*n*
unintended consequences of, 72–77
medical marijuana, xvii–xviii, 30–31,
39–44, 103–4
access to children and teens, 37–38,
40–42
lack of regulation, xvii–xviii, 50–53
marketing of, 45–47, 49
teen drug-related suspensions/
expulsions, 40–41, *41*
THC extraction lab explosion injuries,
73–74, *74*
Colorado Department of Education, 40
Colorado Department of Public Health and
Environment, 103–4
Columbia University, 15, 41, 89
Commerce Clause, 163
Compassionate Investigational New Drug
program, 65–66
CompStat, 124, 124*n*
Compton, Wilson, 181–92
Conservative Political Action Conference
(CPAC), 3
conservatives, legalization support by, 3,
83, 84–86, 162–63
Constitution, U.S., 32
Controlled Substances Act (CSA), 32
Cowan, Richard, 69
crack, 47*n*
crime and marijuana, 100–104
arrests, 95–100, 104, 168–69
interdiction seizures, 42–43, *43,*
161–62
property crime, 85–86

cultural acceptance of marijuana, xviii,
10–12, 116–17, 177–78
drug use and stigmatization, 7–10
Hollywood's role, 117–18, 119–23
polling data, xvi–xvii, 142–43
President Obama and, 2–3, 116–17
CVS, tobacco sales, 155

dabbing, 73
decriminalization of marijuana. *See*
legalization of marijuana; *and
specific countries and states*
Denver Post, 38, 101–2
depression, as adverse effect of marijuana
use, 26, 57, 147
DiSalvo, David, 72
dispensaries, 30–31, 34–35, 39–40, 175
lack of regulation of, 50–53
marketing of medical marijuana by,
44–50
distributors/dealers, 100–104
District of Columbia
marijuana legalization, xviii, 31
medical marijuana, xviii, 9–10, 30
doctors, recommendation notes or letters
for medical marijuana, xvii, 34,
35–36, 60
dog poisonings, 44
dopamine, 6, 15
Dowd, Maureen, 71–72, 168, 171–72
driving accidents/deaths, and marijuana
use, 26–27, 28, 74–75, 87, 88, 92,
141, 166, 176, 184–85
dronabinol (Marinol), 62–64, 67–68
drug cartels and legalization, 100–104
Drug Enforcement Administration (DEA),
34, 65, 67*n,* 120, 197*n*
Drug Policy Alliance, 155–56
drugs, FDA-approved marijuana, 62–64
Drugs and Drug Policy (Kleiman,
Caulkins, and Hawken), 80–81
drug tourists
in Colorado, 42–43, 86–88
in the Netherlands, 126–27, 128
drug trafficking, 100–104
drug use and abuse, 24–25, 110–24.
See also addiction

About the Authors

William J. Bennett

William J. Bennett is one of America's most important, influential, and respected voices on cultural, political, and education issues. A native of Brooklyn, New York, Bill Bennett studied philosophy at Williams College (B.A.) and the University of Texas (Ph.D.) and earned a law degree (J.D.) from Harvard. He is the Washington Fellow of the Claremont Institute.

Dr. Bennett has succeeded in a trifecta of American institutions. He is an award-winning professor in academia, having taught at Boston University, the University of Texas, and Harvard; he is a three-time confirmed executive in the Ronald Reagan and George H. W. Bush administrations including holding two cabinet-level positions, Secretary of Education under Ronald Reagan and the nation's first Drug Czar under the first President Bush; he is the author of more than twenty-four books, including two *New York Times* number one best sellers and two of the most successful books of the 1990s; and he is the host of the number seven ranked nationally syndicated radio show, *Morning in America*.

Dr. Bennett is perceived—even by his adversaries—as a man of strong, reasoned convictions who speaks candidly, eloquently, and honestly about some of the most important issues of our time.

Robert A. White, Esq.

Robert A. White is an attorney who spent his forty-plus year career specializing in commercial litigation. Immediately after he graduated from Columbia University School of Law, he was an Assistant United States Attorney in the District of New Jersey. He subsequently entered private practice, and for almost twenty years was the managing partner of the Princeton, NJ office of a large international law firm. His academic experience includes serving as an Adjunct Assistant Professor, Department of Environmental and Community Medicine, University of Medicine and Dentistry—Rutgers University Medical School, and Adjunct Instructor at Seton Hall University School of Law.